best ever

baking

p

This is a Parragon Publishing Book
First published in 2003

Parragon Publishing
Queen Street House
4 Queen Street
Bath BA1 1HE
United Kingdom

Created and produced by
The Bridgewater Book Company Ltd,
Lewes, East Sussex

Photographer Ian Parsons
Home Economists Sara Hesketh & Richard Green

ISBN: 1-40542-044-8

Printed in China

NOTE

This book uses imperial, metric, or US cup measurements. Follow the same units
of measurement throughout; do not mix imperial and metric. All spoon
measurements are level: teaspoons are assumed to be 5 ml and tablespoons
are assumed to be 15 ml. Unless otherwise stated, milk is assumed to be whole
milk, eggs and individual fruits such as bananas are medium, and pepper is
freshly ground black pepper.

The times given for each recipe are an approximate guide only because
the preparation times may differ according to the techniques used by
different people and the cooking times may vary as a result of the type of
oven used. Ovens should be preheated to the specified temperature. If using
a fan-assisted oven, check the manufacturer's instructions for adjusting the time
and temperature. The preparation times include chilling and marinating times,
where appropriate.

The nutritional information provided for each recipe is per serving or
per portion. Optional ingredients, variations, or serving suggestions have
not been included in the calculations.

Recipes using raw or very lightly cooked eggs should be avoided
by infants, the elderly, pregnant women, convalescents, and anyone
suffering from an illness.

contents

introduction

Baking is generally taken to mean the preparation of flour-based goods such as cakes, bread, tarts, and cookies, which are then cooked in an oven or, occasionally, on a griddle. The delicious, homemade food that results makes the effort in the kitchen worth while—particularly when it is served warm, straight from the oven. Baking also fills the kitchen with appetizing aromas, and can be one of the most satisfying tasks, even for the reluctant cook!

The first ovens were wood-fired and were confined to relatively wealthy households. Poorer families baked on griddles or in Dutch ovens on top of a fire, or they might have sent the dough to a public bakehouse. Coal-fired ranges were developed in the nineteenth century, then gas and electric ovens were gradually introduced into modern kitchens in the twentieth century. Home baking was always a very important part of domestic life, but times have changed and the traditional weekly baking day is a thing of the past. Traditionally it was women who did the home baking, but nowadays most women work and do not have time to bake on a regular basis. Also, eating habits have changed and we have forgone the pleasure of large meals ending with a pie or dessert. Most significantly, children no longer learn traditional cooking skills at school or in the kitchen at home.

However, there are signs that things are changing and we are rediscovering the art of baking as a pleasurable, satisfying, and relaxing leisure activity. Modern equipment and ingredients, as well as a taste for less elaborate cakes and desserts, mean that anyone can produce delicious and impressive dishes with a minimum of effort.

electrical equipment

food processor: These have a multitude of uses, from mixing cake batters and pie dough to kneading dough for bread, as well as chopping nuts and fruit, grating chocolate, and puréeing fruit.

electric mixer: If you do a lot of baking, an electric mixer is invaluable. It can cope with large quantities and is better at creaming than a food processor. It is able to incorporate more air when whisking and can therefore be used for whisked cake batters and for beating egg whites for meringues. It will also fold ingredients such as nuts and fruit into a mixture without chopping them.

electric hand-mixer: These are inexpensive and take the hard work out of creaming small quantities, whisking egg whites, and whipping cream.

bread-making machine: These have recently become extremely popular. They mix, knead, and bake the bread, but if you wish to shape your own bread, make bread rolls, or add extra ingredients before baking, you can still use the machine for mixing and kneading the dough.

measuring equipment

scales: When baking, it is important to measure the ingredients accurately. Reliable scales are essential and there are several types available. Electronic scales are the most accurate, particularly for weighing small quantities. They usually have a switch that allows you to select imperial or metric measurements, and you can set them back to zero after each addition when adding ingredients to a bowl, pan, or pitcher. Traditional balance scales are sturdy and accurate, but it is not always easy to be precise when measuring very small quantities. Sets of weights

are available in either imperial or metric. Spring-balance scales are less hard-wearing and they tend to be light, which makes them easy to knock over; if buying this type, choose one that has both imperial and metric measurements clearly marked.

measuring cups and spoons: A reliable set of measuring cups is just as essential as a good set of scales. Measuring spoons are also available, in sets graduating from ⅛ teaspoon to 1 tablespoon. These are precise measurements; for example, 1 teaspoon = 5 ml. Measuring spoons should be used in preference to domestic spoons, which vary considerably in capacity. Unless otherwise stated, spoon measurements given in recipes are assumed to be level.

measuring pitchers: A clear, heatproof pitcher showing both imperial and metric measurements is the best choice, because the measurements will be easy to read and the pitcher can be put in the microwave if you are heating milk or melting butter. It is a good idea to buy two pitchers in different sizes—a small pitcher is essential for measuring small amounts of liquid, which tend to get lost at the bottom of a large pitcher.

baking equipment

When buying any equipment, choose the best you can afford. This is especially true of cake pans, tart pans, and cookie sheets. Cheap ones tend to be flimsy and can warp and buckle in the heat of the oven. Good-quality pans are solid and hard-wearing and conduct the heat evenly. Care should be taken when washing, drying, and storing the pans. If the pans have a nonstick coating, it is important to wash them thoroughly in hot soapy water, otherwise a layer of grease will build up on the surface, rendering the coating less effective. Avoid using metal tools on a nonstick coating, because they will scratch the surface. It is important to dry traditional pans thoroughly after washing, to avoid rusting—it is a good idea to leave them in a cooling oven. Anodized aluminum is becoming popular and makes very good-quality, strong pans which will not rust and which conduct the heat well.

cake pans: Sponge cake pans should be bought in pairs, and 7-inch/18-cm and 8-inch/20-cm pans will be the most useful sizes. Deep round pans of the same diameters will be needed for fruit cakes. Like sponge cake pans, they may have fixed or loose bottoms, and may or may not have a nonstick coating. Deep square pans can be used instead of round pans for a variety of cakes, especially fruit cakes. Shallower square or rectangular pans are ideal for tray-bakes, brownies, and layered pastries such as baklava. Springform pans with a metal clip that releases the sides are ideal for cheesecakes or any other cakes, which may be particularly fragile or have a crumble topping that you will not want to invert. There are also a variety of ring

molds, kugelhopf pans, and angel food cake pans, which have a hole in the center. They make attractive cakes, but an ordinary round pan can be made into a ring mold by placing a can in the center. Some springform pans come with a variety of different bottoms, one of which will have a funnel in the center.

loaf pans: Rectangular loaf pans are available in 1-lb/450-g and 2-lb/900-g sizes. Apart from their use in bread-making, they are ideal for teabreads and, in fact, almost any cake recipe can be baked in them when you want a loaf-shaped, easy-to-slice cake.

cookie sheets and jelly roll pans: Strong cookie sheets are essential for cookies, meringues, choux pastries, and biscuits. Standing pies and tarts on a preheated cookie sheet while baking will ensure that the shell will be crisp. They are usually completely flat with one raised edge, which makes it easy to slide off tarts and biscuits. It is a good idea to have two or three so that you can bake quantities of pastries and cookies at one time. The most useful sizes are 8 x 12 inches/20 x 30 cm, 10 x 14 inches/ 25 x 35 cm, and 11 x 16 inches/28 x 40 cm.

tart pans: Loose-bottom pans with fluted sides are available in a wide range of sizes and depths. Those sold as tart pans are shallower than quiche pans. Professional cooks tend to use tart rings, which simply sit on a flat cookie sheet. These can be either plain or fluted. Strictly speaking, fluted rings should be used for sweet tarts and plain rings for savory tarts and quiches.

patty pans: Six- and twelve-hole patty pans come in a variety of sizes. There are deep pans for large or mini muffins, and shallower ones for tartlets, mini quiches, and fairy cakes. In good cooking equipment stores, you will also find a variety of individual tart pans in a range of shapes for miniature savories.

additional equipment

There is no limit to the equipment that could accumulate in your kitchen cupboards and drawers, most of which might never be used, but there are some items that are essential for making your time in the kitchen as easy and efficient as possible.

cooling racks: It is important to place cakes and cookies on wire racks to cool. This allows the air to circulate underneath, preventing the underside becoming moist and heavy. If you make quantities of cookies, you will need several of these.

strainer: A strainer is necessary for sifting flour, confectioners' sugar, unsweetened cocoa, spices, and baking powder. Sifting not only removes lumps, but also helps to incorporate air, making the mixture lighter. A miniature strainer is useful for dusting confectioners' sugar or unsweetened cocoa over a cake. Strainers are also used for straining custards before they are cooked, or for removing solid flavorings such as orange peel or vanilla beans after infusing milk. For straining fruit purées, you will need a stainless steel or nylon strainer.

mixing bowls: Choose large bowls, which allow you the space to incorporate plenty of air when creaming cake batters or whisking egg whites. Large bowls are also essential for bread-making, so that there is room for the dough to rise. China or glass bowls are preferable to plastic ones, as it is easier to ensure that they are spotlessly clean and greasefree, which is important when making meringue.

rolling pin: This should be at least 20-inches/50-cm long, made of wood, completely smooth, and straight at the ends with no handles. A good rolling pin is essential for rolling out dough and cookies and, when oiled, is perfect for shaping tuiles and other curled cookies.

cutters: A set of plain or fluted cutters in a variety of sizes is essential for cutting out dough, cookies, and biscuits, and a few shaped cutters are also needed for cookie-making, particularly at Christmas, or if you do baking with children. Cutters are either metal or plastic, and while plastic cutters are safer for children, metal ones cut more precisely, without dragging. This is especially important when using puff pastry, as it will not rise properly if it has not been cut neatly.

pastry bags: Nylon pastry bags are available in a range of sizes. They are strong and can be washed and reused. You will need a fairly large bag for handling cream, meringues, choux pastry, and cookie batters. For decorations, you can make a small pastry bag out of waxed paper, or simply snip a corner off a small plastic bag.

nozzles: A large plain and a large star nozzle are the most useful for cream, meringues, choux pastry, and cookie batters. Smaller nozzles, with an adaptor to fit them into a pastry bag, will be useful if you intend to do much in the way of cake decorating.

graters: Box graters with a variety of surfaces are the best. They are good for grating cheese, chocolate, citrus zest, gingerroot, and nutmeg. Small graters are useful, especially for nutmeg—particularly the type that have a space in which to store the nutmeg.

dough brushes: These are used for brushing milk or egg over dough or biscuits, moistening the edge of the dough for pies, greasing pans, or brushing a glaze over fruit. Flat brushes are the best for large surfaces while round ones are better for smaller areas. Choose good-quality brushes, because cheaper ones tend to shed their bristles as you brush. Wash them in hot soapy water and rinse well before drying them thoroughly.

tools: Wooden spoons should have long handles and rounded ends. They are ideal for beating, creaming, and stirring in pans. A large metal spoon is essential for folding flour into cake batters and for folding in whisked egg whites. A long-handled, flexible rubber spatula will be needed for scraping batter from the sides of a bowl. Flexible spatulas come in a range of sizes, and are also used for spreading fillings and frostings or for lifting. A balloon whisk is ideal for whisking cream or egg whites or for stirring a sauce to prevent lumps forming. A long serrated knife is useful for slicing cakes into layers, and another useful tool is a combination of serrated knife and spatula. A citrus zester is good for removing zest in delicate, thin strips. A swivel-bladed peeler is ideal for peeling fruit, removing strips of rind, and making chocolate curls.

ingredients

Keep a selection of basic ingredients in the pantry so that you can bake a cake or rustle up a dessert whenever the mood takes you. Buy good-quality ingredients, and keep smaller amounts and replace them often rather than buying large quantities that quickly deteriorate. Store dry goods, such as flour, sugar, dry fruit, and nuts, in a cool place in airtight containers.

flour: Flour provides the structure that holds the ingredients together, so it is important to choose the right kind. The way in which flours perform in cooking varies according to their ability to form gluten. Strong all-purpose flour is high in gluten and is used in bread-making. It is also good for choux pastry.

All-purpose flour is used for dough, most cookies, rich fruit cakes, and whisked sponges. It is also used in cakes that include whisked egg whites, as the air in the egg whites causes the batter to rise. All-purpose flour can be made into self-rising flour by adding baking powder: generally, 4 teaspoons of baking powder to 1 lb/450 g flour. Whole-wheat flour can be used instead of white flour in some cakes, but it gives a heavier texture and is often combined with white flour. After sifting whole-wheat flour, add the bran that remains in the sifter.

Buckwheat flour is strong and dark and is traditionally used, combined with white flour, in blinis. Cornstarch is a fine maize flour that gives a short texture to cookies such as Mexican Pastelitos (see page 36). It is also added to the egg whites when making a pavlova or meringue roulade, to give the center of the meringue a light, chewy texture. Cornmeal is usually combined with all-purpose flour and gives a yellow color and a crunchy, open texture to cakes, muffins, and cornbread. Semolina is used in a similar way; it is fine-grained and rich in protein and starch. It gives a good open texture to Moroccan Orange & Almond Cake (see page 226), which allows it to absorb the warm syrup that is poured over after baking.

raising agents: Baking powder is a mixture of cream of tartar and baking soda, which produces carbon dioxide, causing a mixture to rise. It starts to work as soon as it is added to liquid, which is why a cake batter should be put in the oven as quickly as possible. When making a cake by the all-in-one method, you will add extra baking powder to the self-rising flour to help the cake to rise, because this method does not incorporate as much air as traditional creaming. Extra baking powder is also added to a biscuit dough. Sometimes baking soda is used on its own to give heavy mixtures a lift, especially when the mixture has a spicy flavor, such as in Gingerbread People (see page 16). Yeast is used to make bread dough rise, as it produces carbon dioxide during rising. Purists may favor fresh yeast when baking bread, but the active dry yeasts are more widely available, convenient, and easy to use, and produce excellent results.

sweeteners: Unrefined sugar is best for all baking and is used in most of the recipes in this book. It retains the sugar cane's natural molasses to give a smooth, mellow, and rounded flavor. Superfine sugar is used most frequently in these recipes. It is a fine-grained sugar with a subtle taste and it creams easily with butter and dissolves quickly when beaten with eggs. In both cases, superfine sugar helps the mixture retain air. In melted cake batters, granulated or raw brown sugar can be used because the sugar is dissolved in the early stages.

Some recipes use ordinary brown sugar. This is soft and moist with a full, rich flavor, but it tends to form into clumps in the package and may need to be strained before use. Confectioners' sugar is a fine, powdery sugar for frosting and buttercream fillings. It can also be used to sweeten pastry and makes a decorative topping when sifted over cakes and desserts. Unrefined confectioners'

sugar has a golden color, so refined confectioners' sugar is best for pure white frosting. Confectioners' sugar should always be sifted before use. Some recipes use corn syrup, molasses, honey, or maple syrup to add sweetness.

eggs: Unless otherwise stated, medium eggs are used in these recipes. For the best flavor, choose organic eggs. Eggs aerate a cake and provide richness and flavor. They will keep in the refrigerator for 1–2 weeks, but should be allowed to come to room temperature before use in order to achieve the best aeration. Alternatively, place the cold eggs into the mixing bowl and cover with warm water. By the time you have weighed all the other ingredients, the eggs will be at the right temperature and the bowl will be pleasantly warm for mixing the cake.

dairy produce and fats: Butter is used in most of the recipes in this book, as it gives the best flavor. However, if you prefer not to use butter, substitute a good-quality margarine. For all-in-one cake batters, choose a soft margarine that is especially for baking. Lowfat spreads are not a suitable alternative. Butter will keep in the refrigerator for 2–3 weeks, but it should be allowed to come to room temperature before rubbing in or creaming.

Where a recipe says "butter, softened" it means that the butter has been out of the refrigerator for as long as it takes for it to become soft enough to cream easily. Use lightly salted butter for cakes, dough, and cookies and sweet for cake fillings and frostings. Butter is used in unsweetened pie dough to add flavor, but white cooking fat is usually added to make the pastry crisp.

Heavy cream is used in several of the recipes in this book. It contains a high percentage of fat, which enables it to be whipped firmly. Whipping cream is not a good substitute, as it does not hold its volume for as long as heavy cream.

Sour cream is included in the filling for the Peach Melba Meringue Roulade (see page 240), as its sourness is a good contrast to the sweetness of the meringue. Mascarpone is an Italian cream cheese that makes a rich filling for the Strawberry & Almond Roulade (see page 237). Cream cheese is an essential ingredient in the classic Manhattan Cheesecake (see page 234), and the sour cream that is also in this recipe is a foil to its richness. Buttermilk is a traditional ingredient in biscuits and its sourness helps them to rise.

nuts and fruit: Buy nuts in small quantities, as they become rancid and bitter after 3–4 months. Ground nuts lose their flavor even more quickly. If you buy unblanched almonds, they need to be blanched before use. Simply pour boiling water over them and leave for a few minutes; the brown skins will then slip off easily. To remove the brown skins from hazelnuts, heat them on a cookie sheet in the oven, or in a dry skillet, for a few minutes, then place them in a clean, dry dish towel and rub vigorously to remove the skins. Roasting nuts such as hazelnuts, almonds, and pine nuts in a dry skillet brings out their rich flavor, but it is easy to burn them, as they contain a lot of oil. Freshly grated coconut adds moisture to cakes, and toasted coconut shavings make an attractive decoration.

Dry fruits are used in many of the recipes in this book, and for decorating cakes. They should be stored in airtight containers, as they can dry out if not stored carefully. Most dry fruit, such as raisins, will benefit from being plumped up by soaking overnight in orange juice, brandy, or even hot water. Ready-to-eat dried fruits have already been soaked and are moist and soft. If you are using candied peel, it is always better to buy the pieces of fruit and chop them yourself rather than buy the pots of ready-chopped peel.

flavorings: If possible, it is always better to buy whole spices and grind them yourself, as they quickly lose their flavor once they have been ground. However, some spices, such as cinnamon, are difficult to grind at home. If you buy ready-ground spices, use them up quickly, and store them in the pantry rather than on the counter.

Vanilla beans should be sticky and pliable. Keep them in a jar of superfine sugar and use the flavored sugar when baking. As an alternative to vanilla beans, use liquid vanilla extract, which is made by macerating crushed vanilla beans in alcohol. Vanilla flavoring is synthetic and is not a good substitute. Orange-flower and rose water are strongly perfumed distilled flower essences that add an exotic flavor to cakes and syrups.

baking essentials

oven temperature: Oven temperatures vary so the recommended cooking times in recipes are guidelines only. The oven temperatures in this book are for a conventional oven. If you have a fan oven, consult the handbook, as the cooking times may be considerably shorter and the temperature may need to be reduced. It is important to preheat the oven before baking and for most purposes the oven shelf should be placed in the center. In fan ovens the temperature is even throughout the oven, which is ideal for batch baking.

preparing cake pans: It is important to use the right size and shape of pan, though if you do not have quite the right size pan, it means that the cooking time will need adjusting. For instance, if the cake pan is slightly bigger than suggested in the recipe, the cake will be thinner and will cook more quickly.

It is worth taking time to prepare the pan before use to stop the cake from sticking. Unusually shaped pans need to be brushed with oil or melted butter and dusted with flour. Round, square, or rectangular pans can be lined with nonstick parchment paper or greased waxed paper. To prevent rich fruit cakes becoming too brown and drying out at the edges during cooking, secure a thick band of brown paper round the outside of the cake pan.

To line a round or square cake pan, brush the inside evenly with oil or melted butter. Cut a strip of paper, 2 inches/5 cm wider than the depth of the pan, to fit round the sides and overlap. Fold in one long edge of the paper by 1 inch/2.5 cm and crease. Unfold and make cuts at 1-inch/2.5-cm intervals along the edge up to the crease. Place the paper strip in the pan so that the creased edge rests in the join at the bottom. Press into place on the greased sides and bottom of the pan. Place the pan on another sheet of paper and draw a pencil line round the bottom. Cut out the circle or square just inside the line and lay in the bottom of the pan.

To line a small square or loaf pan, place the pan on a sheet of paper, large enough to extend up the sides and beyond them by 1 inch/2.5 cm. Draw a pencil line round the bottom and crease along the lines. From the longer edges, cut along the creases up to the marked lines. Grease the pan and line with the paper, tucking the flaps behind the longer sides.

For many recipes it is necessary only to grease and line the bottom of the pans with a paper circle or square. For loaf pans, line a greased pan with a strip of paper the width of the pan which extends up the short ends.

separating eggs: Carefully crack the shell on the edge of a clean bowl. Gently prise the shell apart in two halves, taking care not to split the yolk. Quickly pass the egg yolk from one half shell to the other, letting the white fall into the bowl below.

melting chocolate: Care must be taken when melting chocolate to make sure that it does not become overheated. The most reliable method is to put the chocolate in a bowl set over a pan of simmering water, making sure that the bottom of the bowl does not come into contact with the water. Remove the pan from the heat and leave until the chocolate has melted.

basic methods

cake-making: Many cakes in this book are made either by the creamed method or the all-in-one method. In creamed cakes, vigorous "creaming" of the butter, sugar, and eggs incorporates the air that is essential to produce a good cake. For best results, the ingredients should be at room temperature. First of all, beat the butter until soft and creamy, then add the sugar, and beat until light and fluffy and doubled in volume. The beaten eggs are added a little at a time, beating well between each addition. If the batter curdles, it will not hold as much air, so if it looks as if it might curdle, stir in a little of the flour. The flour should be folded in with a figure-of-eight movement with a large metal spoon. Do not stir or beat the batter, otherwise the added air will be lost. The batter should be smooth and creamy and drop reluctantly from a spoon. If it seems too stiff, add a little milk. The batter may be creamed in a mixer, or in a bowl with a hand-mixer.

As the name of the method suggests, when making all-in-one cakes, all the ingredients are put in a bowl together and beaten until smooth. This is easy and quick if done in a food processor. Extra baking powder is added to compensate for the fact that this method does not incorporate as much air as the creaming method.

turning out and storing cakes: A cooked sponge will look well-risen and golden. The edge of the cake will be just starting to shrink away from the sides of the pan. The cake should also feel springy when you press the center lightly with your fingertips. A fine skewer or the tip of a knife inserted in the center of the cake should come out clean and not sticky, though this is not a reliable test for cakes that contain fruit. Let the cake rest in the pan for a few minutes. If the sides of the pan are unlined, run a knife round the inside edge of the pan to loosen it. Turn the cake out onto a cooling rack and, if necessary, peel off the lining paper on the bottom. Let cool completely before decorating or storing.

To store undecorated cakes, wrap in waxed paper and foil, then store in an airtight container. To freeze, place the wrapped cake in a freezer bag, remove the air, then seal, label, and date. Thaw, still wrapped, in a cool place. Cakes filled with cream or chocolate should be kept in an airtight plastic box in the refrigerator. Other layered cakes must be kept in a cool place.

dough

It can be quite a time-consuming and skilful job to make flaky or phyllo pastry successfully, and because they are widely available in either the freezer or chiller cabinets in food stores, the recipes in this book use ready-made puff and phyllo pastry. You can also buy good-quality, ready-made unsweetened and sweet pie dough, and they are very useful when time is short. However, they are not difficult to make at home, so some basic recipes are given on the page opposite.

When you are making dough, make sure that you keep everything as cool as possible, and try to avoid handling it more than necessary. For this reason, dough made in a food processor is particularly successful. Follow the manufacturer's instructions for making dough in a food processor. To make whole-wheat dough, replace half the white flour with whole-wheat flour.

basic recipes

unsweetened pie dough

makes: 1 x 6-inch/15-cm tart shell
preparation time: 10 minutes,
plus 30 minutes chilling

generous ¾ cup all-purpose flour
2 tbsp butter
2 tbsp white cooking fat
2 tbsp cold water

1 Sift the flour into a mixing bowl.
Cut the butter and fat into small
cubes and add them to the flour. Using
your fingertips, gently rub the fats and
flour together until the fat breaks down
into tiny pieces and the mixture resembles
fine bread crumbs. This should be done as
quickly and lightly as possible.

2 Stir in most of the water with a
round-bladed knife. You may not
need all the liquid, as the absorbency of
flour varies. Alternatively, you may need to
add a little extra liquid. Gather the dough
into a ball and knead briefly. If it feels
sticky, sprinkle over a little flour. Wrap the
dough in plastic wrap and let chill in the
refrigerator for about 30 minutes.

sweet pie dough

makes: 1 x 8-inch/20-cm tart shell
preparation time: 10 minutes,
plus 30 minutes chilling

generous 1½ cups all-purpose flour
½ cup butter
1 tbsp white cooking fat
¼ cup golden superfine sugar
6 tbsp cold milk

Make in the same way as unsweetened
pie dough, stirring in the superfine
sugar after you have rubbed the
butter and fat into the flour, and
using milk instead of water.

pâte sucrée

makes: 1 x 8-inch/20-cm tart shell
preparation time: 10 minutes,
plus 30 minutes chilling

generous 1½ cups all-purpose flour
½ cup butter, chilled and cubed
¼ cup golden superfine sugar
1 egg yolk
1 tsp vanilla extract
a little water (optional)

Make in the same way as unsweetened pie
dough, stirring in the sugar after you have
rubbed the butter into the flour. Stir in the
egg yolk and vanilla extract with a little
water to form a smooth dough.

rolling out dough: Sprinkle a little flour
on a counter and the rolling pin, then roll
out the dough, rolling away from you in
one direction, using even pressure. Turn
the dough a quarter turn, counter-
clockwise, occasionally. Do not pull or
stretch the dough.

to line a tart pan: Roll out the dough
until it is about 2 inches/5 cm larger than
the tart pan all round. Use the rolling pin
to help you lift the dough over the pan.

Lift the edges of the dough so that it falls
down into the pan. Press it gently, without
stretching, against the edges of the pan.
Turn any surplus dough outward over the
rim and roll the rolling pin over the top to
cut off the surplus. If possible, chill for an
additional 30 minutes.

baking blind: Lightly prick the chilled tart
shell, then line with a large sheet of waxed
paper or foil. Fill with dried beans or pie
weights. Bake in a preheated oven at
400°F/200°C for 10–15 minutes, or until
the dough looks "set." Carefully remove
the paper and dried beans or weights and
return to the oven for an additional
5–10 minutes, or until the bottom is firm
to the touch and light golden.

cookies & crackers

*There are many occasions when it is good to have a store of homemade cookies
in the kitchen cupboard: when friends drop in for a chat, after school when hungry children
need re-fuelling, to pop in lunch boxes, or just for those times when you fancy a little
something with a cup of coffee.*

*You do not need to be an experienced cook to be able to make successful cookies,
because they are surprisingly easy to make and require little, or no, special equipment.
You can produce cookies at home for a fraction of the cost of store-bought ones,
and not only do they cost less, they taste better too!*

*In this section you will find recipes for a whole variety of cookies, from homely
and chunky treats, such as Oatie Pecan Cookies (see page 24) or Double Chocolate Chip
Cookies (see page 32), to light cookies with delicate flavors, such as Lavender Cookies (see
page 37) or Pistachio & Cardamom Tuiles (see page 29), which are perfect for serving with ice
cream. Children will enjoy making (and eating) Gingerbread People (see page 16) or Party
Cookies (see page 22), and there are special cookies such as Almond Biscotti (see page 28),
which make an ideal accompaniment to after-dinner coffee. As well as sweet cookies,
there are recipes for savory crackers such as Spiced Cocktail Bites (see page 42)
and Pesto Palmiers (see page 46), for serving with drinks.*

gingerbread people

makes 20, using large cutters

prep: 30 mins, plus 30 mins cooling

cook: 15–20 mins

These are a favorite with children, who love to make the gingerbread shapes. The recipe makes a pliable dough that is easy to handle.

INGREDIENTS

½ cup butter, plus
extra for greasing

3½ cups all-purpose flour,
plus extra for dusting

2 tsp ground ginger

1 tsp allspice

2 tsp baking soda

generous ⅓ cup corn syrup

generous ½ cup brown sugar

1 egg, beaten

TO DECORATE

currants

candied cherries

generous ¾ cup confectioners' sugar

3–4 tsp water

NUTRITIONAL INFORMATION

Calories 71

Protein 1g

Carbohydrate 13g

Sugars 6g

Fat 2g

Saturates 1g

variation

The gingerbread dough can be cut into whatever shapes you prefer, so experiment with some creative ideas.

cook's tip

At Christmas, cut out star and bell shapes. When the cookies come out of the oven, gently pierce a hole in each one with a skewer. Thread ribbons through and hang on the Christmas tree.

1 Preheat the oven to 325°F/160°C, then grease 3 large cookie sheets. Sift the flour, ginger, allspice, and baking soda into a large bowl. Place the butter, syrup, and sugar in a pan over low heat and stir until melted. Pour onto the dry ingredients and add the egg. Mix together to form a dough. The dough will be sticky to start with, but will become firmer as it cools.

2 On a lightly floured counter, roll out the dough to about ⅛-inch/ 3-mm thick and stamp out gingerbread people shapes. Place on the prepared cookie sheets. Re-knead and re-roll the trimmings and cut out more shapes until the dough is used up. Decorate with currants for eyes and pieces of cherry for mouths. Bake in the oven for 15–20 minutes, or until firm and lightly browned.

3 Remove from the oven and let cool on the cookie sheets for a few minutes, then transfer to wire racks to cool completely. Mix the confectioners' sugar with the water to a thick consistency. Place the frosting in a small plastic bag and cut a tiny hole in one corner. Use the frosting to draw buttons or clothes shapes on the cooled cookies.

spiced cookies

prep: 15 mins, plus
20 mins cooling

cook: 12 mins

These spicy cookies are perfect to serve with fruit salad or ice cream for a very easy instant dessert.

INGREDIENTS

6 oz/175 g unsalted butter, plus extra
for greasing

scant ⅞ cup brown sugar

1½ cups all-purpose flour

pinch of salt

½ tsp baking soda

1 tsp ground cinnamon

½ tsp ground coriander

½ tsp ground nutmeg

¼ tsp ground cloves

2 tbsp dark rum

NUTRITIONAL INFORMATION

Calories	.117
Protein	.1g
Carbohydrate	.15g
Sugars	.8g
Fat	.6g
Saturates	.4g

cook's tip

Use the back of a fork or spoon to flatten the cookies slightly before baking. After baking, carefully transfer the cookies to wire racks, otherwise they may fall apart.

1 Preheat the oven to 350°F/180°C. Grease 2 cookie sheets. Beat the butter and sugar together, then whisk until light and fluffy.

2 Sift the flour, salt, baking soda, cinnamon, coriander, nutmeg, and cloves into the batter. Stir in the dark rum.

3 Using 2 teaspoons, place small mounds of the batter, onto the cookie sheets, placing them 3 inches/7.5 cm apart to allow for spreading during cooking. Flatten each one slightly with the back of a spoon.

4 Bake in the preheated oven for 10–12 minutes, or until golden. Transfer the cookies to wire racks to cool completely and crispen before serving.

savory curried cookies

cook: 15 mins

prep: 15 mins, plus 20 mins cooling

makes 13

When making these cookies, try different types of curry powder strengths until you find the one that suits your own taste.

NUTRITIONAL INFORMATION

Calories 48

Protein 2g

Carbohydrate 2g

Sugars 0g

Fat 12g

Saturates 2g

INGREDIENTS

3½ oz/100 g butter, softened, plus extra for greasing

scant ¾ cup all-purpose flour, plus extra for dusting

1 tsp salt

2 tsp curry powder

⅞ cup Cheshire cheese, grated

⅞ cup freshly grated Parmesan cheese

1 Preheat the oven to 350°F/180°C, then lightly grease 4 cookie sheets. Sift the flour and salt into a large bowl. Stir in the curry powder and the grated Cheshire and Parmesan cheeses. Rub in the softened butter with your fingertips until the mixture comes together to form a soft dough.

2 Roll out the dough thinly on a lightly floured counter, to form a rectangle. Using a 2-inch/5-cm cookie cutter, cut out 40 round cookies. Arrange the cookies on the prepared cookie sheets.

3 Bake in the preheated oven for 10–15 minutes, or until golden brown. Let the cookies cool slightly on the cookie sheets. Carefully transfer the cookies to a wire rack and let stand until completely cold and crisp, then serve.

cook's tip

Make sure the cookies are completely cold and crisp before storing in an airtight, plastic container. These cookies can be stored for several days .

shortbread fantails

makes 8　　　　**prep: 10 mins, plus ⟳
30 mins cooling**　　　　**cook: 15 mins ⟳**

*These elegant cookies are perfect for afternoon tea or they
can be served with ice cream for a delicious dessert.*

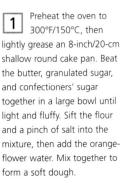

INGREDIENTS

4½ oz/125 g butter, softened, plus extra
for greasing

scant ¼ cup granulated sugar

generous ⅛ cup confectioners' sugar

1½ cups all-purpose flour, plus
extra for dusting

salt

2 tsp orange-flower water

superfine sugar, for sprinkling

NUTRITIONAL INFORMATION

Calories	.248
Protein	.3g
Carbohydrate	.32g
Sugars	.10g
Fat	.13g
Saturates	.9g

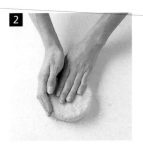

cook's tip

For a crunchy addition,
sprinkle 2 tablespoons of
chopped mixed nuts over
the top of the fantails
before baking.

1 Preheat the oven to
300°F/150°C, then
lightly grease an 8-inch/20-cm
shallow round cake pan. Beat
the butter, granulated sugar,
and confectioners' sugar
together in a large bowl until
light and fluffy. Sift the flour
and a pinch of salt into the
mixture, then add the orange-
flower water. Mix together to
form a soft dough.

2 Roll out the dough
on a lightly floured
counter, to an 8-inch/20-cm
circle and place in the prepared
pan. Prick the dough well and
score into 8 triangles with a
round-bladed knife.

3 Bake in the oven for
30–35 minutes, or until
the shortbread is crisp and a
pale golden color.

4 Sprinkle with superfine
sugar, then cut along
the marked lines to make
the 8 fantails. Let the
shortbread cool before
removing the pieces from
the pan. Store in an airtight
container for several days.

vanilla hearts

cook: 20 mins

prep: 10 mins, plus 30 mins cooling

makes 12

This is a classic shortbread cookie which melts in the mouth. Here the cookies are made in pretty heart shapes.

NUTRITIONAL INFORMATION	
Calories	150
Protein	1g
Carbohydrate	20g
Sugars	9g
Fat	8g
Saturates	5g

INGREDIENTS

5½ oz/150 g butter, cut into small pieces, plus extra for greasing

1½ cups all-purpose flour, plus extra for dusting

1⅛ cups superfine sugar, plus extra for dusting

1 tsp vanilla extract

cook's tip

Place a fresh vanilla bean in your superfine sugar and keep it in a storage jar for several weeks to give the sugar a delicious vanilla flavor.

1 Preheat the oven to 350°F/180°C, then lightly grease a cookie sheet. Sift the flour into a large bowl. Add the butter and rub it in with your fingertips until the mixture resembles fine bread crumbs. Stir in the superfine sugar and vanilla extract and mix together to form a firm dough.

2 Roll out the dough on a lightly floured counter to a thickness of 1 inch/2.5 cm. Stamp out 12 hearts with a heart-shaped cookie cutter measuring 2 inches/5 cm across and 1 inch/2.5 cm deep. Arrange the hearts on the prepared cookie sheet.

3 Bake in the preheated oven for 15–20 minutes, or until the hearts are a light golden color. Transfer the vanilla hearts to a wire rack and let cool completely. Dust them with a little superfine sugar just before serving.

party cookies

These cookies are studded with colorful sugar-coated chocolate beans, and are ideal for children's parties.

INGREDIENTS

4 oz/115 g butter, softened, plus extra for greasing

generous ½ cup brown sugar

1 tbsp corn syrup

½ tsp vanilla extract

1¼ cups self-rising flour

3 oz/85 g sugar-coated chocolate beans

NUTRITIONAL INFORMATION

Calories	146
Protein	. . . . .1g
Carbohydrate	. . . . .21g
Sugars	. . . . .12g
Fat	. . . . .7g
Saturates	. . . . .4g

cook's tip

To make a slightly less sugary version of these cookies, you could use chocolate chips, candied cherries or chopped dried apricots instead of the chocolate beans.

1 Preheat the oven to 350°F/180°C, then grease 2 cookie sheets. Place the butter and sugar in a bowl and beat together with an electric whisk until light and fluffy, then beat in the syrup and vanilla extract.

2 Sift in half the flour and work it into the mixture. Stir in the chocolate beans and the remaining flour and work the dough together using a spatular.

3 Roll the dough into 16 balls and place them on the prepared cookie sheets, spaced well apart to allow for spreading. Do not flatten them. Bake in the preheated oven for 10–12 minutes, or until pale golden at the edges. Remove from the oven and let cool on the cookie sheets for 2 minutes, then transfer to wire racks to cool completely.

nutty oat squares

⏲ **cook: 20–25 mins**   ⏰ **prep: 10 mins, plus 30 mins cooling**   **makes 16**

These oat squares are really quick and easy to make. They are perfect for adding to children's lunch boxes.

NUTRITIONAL INFORMATION

Calories 189

Protein 3g

Carbohydrate 19g

Sugars 9g

Fat 12g

Saturates 4g

INGREDIENTS

4 oz/115 g butter, plus

extra for greasing

scant 2¾ cups rolled oats

¾ cup chopped hazelnuts

6 tbsp all-purpose flour

2 tbsp corn syrup

scant ½ cup brown sugar

cook's tip

Be careful not to overcook the mixture, otherwise it is likely to become hard and difficult to cut, rather than deliciously chewy.

1 Preheat the oven to 350°F/180°C, then grease a 9-inch/23-cm square ovenproof dish or cake pan. Place the rolled oats, chopped hazelnuts, and flour in a large mixing bowl and stir together.

2 Place the butter, syrup, and sugar in a pan over low heat and stir until melted. Pour onto the dry ingredients and mix well. Turn into the prepared ovenproof dish and smooth the surface with the back of a spoon.

3 Bake in the oven for 20–25 minutes, or until golden and firm to the touch. Mark into 16 pieces and let cool in the dish. When completely cold, cut through with a sharp knife and remove from the dish.

oatie pecan cookies

makes 15   **prep: 10 mins, plus ↻ 20 mins cooling**   **cook: 15 mins ⏲**

These light, crisp cookies are delicious just as they are, but they also taste exceptionally good served with cheese.

INGREDIENTS

4 oz/115 g butter, softened, plus extra for greasing

scant ½ cup brown sugar

1 egg, beaten

⅓ cup chopped pecans

⅔ cup all-purpose flour

½ tsp baking powder

⅔ cup rolled oats

NUTRITIONAL INFORMATION

Calories 143

Protein 2g

Carbohydrate 13g

Sugars 6g

Fat 10g

Saturates 5g

variation

For a slightly different taste, substitute other chopped nuts, such as walnuts or hazelnuts, for the pecans.

cook's tip

To save a lot of hard work, beat the butter and sugar together with an electric hand-mixer. Alternatively, use a food processor.

1 Preheat the oven to 350°F/180°C, then grease 2 cookie sheets. Place the butter and sugar in a bowl and beat until light and fluffy. Gradually beat in the egg, then stir in the nuts.

2 Sift the flour and baking powder into the mixture and add the oats. Stir together until well combined. Drop spoonfuls of the mixture on to the prepared cookie sheets, spaced well apart to allow for spreading.

3 Bake in the oven for 15 minutes, or until pale golden. Let cool on the cookie sheets for 2 minutes, then transfer to wire racks to cool completely.

ginger-topped fingers

makes 16 | **prep: 15 mins, plus 30 mins cooling** ⏲ | **cook: 40 mins** ♨

Shortbread fingers are always a satisfying treat, but a sticky ginger topping turns them into a real delight.

INGREDIENTS

6 oz/175 g butter, plus extra
for greasing
generous 1½ cups all-purpose flour
1 tsp ground ginger
scant ½ cup golden superfine sugar

GINGER TOPPING

1 tbsp corn syrup
¼ cup butter
2 tbsp confectioners' sugar
1 tsp ground ginger

NUTRITIONAL INFORMATION

Calories 185

Protein 2g

Carbohydrate 19g

Sugars 8g

Fat 12g

Saturates 8g

variation

For decorative effect, draw thin lines of white frosting across the topping before it sets, then drag a toothpick across the lines.

cook's tip

The shortbread will be quite soft when it first comes out of the oven, but it will become firm as it cools. Let these fingers cool completely before serving.

1 Preheat the oven to 350°F/180°C. Grease an 11 x 7-inch/28 x 18-cm rectangular cake pan. Sift the flour and ginger into a bowl and stir in the sugar. Rub in the butter until the cookie dough starts to stick together.

2 Press the cookie dough into the prepared pan and smooth the top with a spatula. Bake in the preheated oven for 40 minutes, or until very lightly browned.

3 To make the topping, place the syrup and butter in a small pan over low heat and stir until melted. Stir in the confectioner's sugar and ginger. Remove the shortbread from the oven and pour the topping over it while both are still hot. Let cool slightly in the pan, then cut into 16 fingers. Transfer to wire racks to cool.

almond biscotti

makes 20–24

prep: 20 mins, plus 20 mins cooling

cook: 25 mins

Biscotti are hard Italian cookies that are traditionally served at the end of a meal for dipping into a sweet white wine, Vin Santo. They are equally delicious served with coffee or to accompany ice cream.

INGREDIENTS

1¾ cups all-purpose flour, plus extra for dusting

1 tsp baking powder

pinch of salt

¾ cup golden superfine sugar

2 eggs, beaten

finely grated rind of 1 unwaxed orange

⅔ cup whole blanched almonds, lightly toasted

NUTRITIONAL INFORMATION

Calories	110
Protein	. . . . .3g
Carbohydrate	. . . . .18g
Sugars	. . . . .8g
Fat	. . . . .4g
Saturates	. . . . .1g

variation

As an alternative to almonds, use hazelnuts or a mixture of almonds and pistachios.

1 Preheat the oven to 350°F/180°C, then lightly dust a cookie sheet with flour. Sift the flour, baking powder, and salt into a bowl. Add the sugar, eggs, and orange rind and mix to a dough, then knead in the toasted almonds.

2 Using your hands, roll the dough into a ball, cut in half, and roll each portion into a log about 1½ inches/4 cm in diameter. Place on the floured cookie sheet and bake in the oven for 10 minutes. Remove from the oven and let cool for 5 minutes.

3 Using a serrated knife, cut the logs into ½-inch/1-cm thick diagonal slices. Arrange the slices on the cookie sheet and return to the oven for 15 minutes, or until slightly golden. Transfer to a wire rack to cool and crispen.

pistachio & cardamom tuiles

cook: 16–30 mins **prep: 15 mins, plus 20 mins cooling** **makes 18**

These wafer-thin, crisp, nutty biscuits are ideal for serving with fresh fruit desserts, or can be used as a delicious alternative to ordinary wafers for scooping up ice cream.

NUTRITIONAL INFORMATION	
Calories 69	
Protein 1g	
Carbohydrate 10g	
Sugars 7g	
Fat 3g	
Saturates 2g	

INGREDIENTS

6 cardamom pods

2 oz/55 g butter, melted and cooled, plus extra for greasing

2 egg whites

generous ½ cup golden superfine sugar

6 tbsp all-purpose flour

scant ¼ cup chopped pistachios

cook's tip

Do not be tempted to bake more than one tray of cookies at a time, otherwise the second batch will become too firm before you have time to shape them.

1 Preheat the oven to 350°F/180°C. Crush the cardamom pods and remove the husks. Grind the black seeds using a mortar and pestle and reserve. Grease 2 or 3 cookie sheets and a rolling pin. Place the egg whites and superfine sugar in a bowl. Whisk together with a fork until frothy.

2 Sift the flour into the bowl. Add the pistachios and ground cardamom and mix with a fork. Add the butter and mix together thoroughly. Drop teaspoons of the mixture on to the prepared cookie sheets, spaced well apart to allow for spreading. Using a spatula, spread each one out slightly.

3 Bake in the preheated oven, 1 sheet at a time, for 8–10 minutes, or until the edges are firm. Lift the cookies off carefully with a spatula and place over the rolling pin while still warm. Let stand to set for 1–2 minutes, then lift off carefully and transfer to a wire rack to cool. Store in an airtight container.

hazelnut squares

makes 16

prep: 15 mins, plus ⏱
20 mins cooling

cook: 25 mins ⏱

These can be made quickly and easily for an afternoon treat. The chopped hazelnuts can be replaced by any other nut of your choice.

INGREDIENTS

3½ oz/100 g butter, cut into small
pieces, plus extra for greasing
generous 1 cup all-purpose flour
salt
1 tsp baking powder
generous ¾ cup firmly packed
brown sugar
1 egg, beaten
4 tbsp milk
generous ¾ cup hazelnuts, halved
raw brown sugar, for sprinkling
(optional)

NUTRITIONAL INFORMATION	
Calories 163
Protein 2g
Carbohydrate 18g
Sugars 10g
Fat 10g
Saturates 4g

1 Preheat the oven to 350°F/180°C. Grease a 9-inch/23-cm square cake pan and line the bottom with parchment paper. Sift the flour, a pinch of salt and the baking powder into a large bowl. Add the butter and rub it in with your fingertips until the mixture resembles fine bread crumbs. Add the brown sugar and stir to mix.

2 Add the egg, milk, and halved hazelnuts to the dry ingredients and stir well until thoroughly combined and the cookie dough is a soft consistency.

3 Spoon the cookie dough into the cake pan and smooth the surface. Sprinkle with raw brown sugar (if using). Bake in the oven for

25 minutes, or until it is firm to the touch when pressed with a finger. Let cool in the pan for 10 minutes, then loosen the edges with a round-bladed knife and turn out onto a wire rack to cool completely. Cut into squares.

variation

For a coffee-time cookie, replace the milk with the same amount of cold strong black coffee—the stronger the better!

cinnamon & seed squares

cook: 45 mins   **prep: 10 mins, plus 1 hr cooling**   **makes 12**

These are moist cake-like squares with a lovely spicy flavor.
They smell simply wonderful while they are cooking.

NUTRITIONAL INFORMATION	
Calories	.397
Protein	.6g
Carbohydrate	.40g
Sugars	.23g
Fat	.25g
Saturates	.14g

INGREDIENTS

9 oz/250 g butter, softened, plus extra
for greasing

generous 1¼ cups superfine sugar

3 eggs, beaten

generous 1⅝ cups self-rising flour

½ tsp baking soda

1 tbsp ground cinnamon

⅔ cup sour cream

scant ½ cup sunflower seeds

cook's tip

These moist squares will freeze
well and will also keep for up
to 1 month in an airtight,
plastic container. If frozen,
make sure they are thoroughly
thawed before eating.

1 Preheat the oven to 350°F/180°C. Grease a 9-inch/23-cm square cake pan and line the bottom with parchment paper. Beat the butter and superfine sugar together in a large bowl until the batter is light and fluffy. Gradually add the beaten eggs to the batter, beating thoroughly after each addition.

2 Sift the self-rising flour, baking soda, and ground cinnamon into the creamed batter and fold in gently, using a metal spoon. Spoon in the sour cream and sunflower seeds and gently mix until well combined.

3 Spoon the batter into the prepared cake pan and smooth the surface with the back of a spoon or a knife. Bake in the preheated oven for 45 minutes, or until the mixture is firm to the touch when pressed with a finger.

4 Loosen the edges with a round-bladed knife, then turn out onto a wire rack to cool completely. Slice into 12 squares.

double chocolate chip cookies

makes 24   **prep: 15 mins, plus** ⏲   **cook: 10–15 mins** ⏲
                      20 mins cooling

These double chocolate cookies, encapsulating pockets of melted chocolate chips, are a melt-in-the-mouth, mid-afternoon treat. They won't be on a plate for long!

INGREDIENTS

4 oz/115 g butter, softened, plus extra for greasing

¼ cup golden superfine sugar

¼ cup brown sugar

1 egg, beaten

½ tsp vanilla extract

generous ¾ cup all-purpose flour

2 tbsp unsweetened cocoa

½ tsp baking soda

⅔ cup milk chocolate chips

⅓ cup coarsely chopped walnuts

NUTRITIONAL INFORMATION	
Calories	116
Protein	2g
Carbohydrate	12g
Sugars	8g
Fat	7g
Saturates	4g

variation

Use semisweet chocolate chips instead of milk chocolate chips, or substitute chopped pecans for the walnuts.

cook's tip

The minimum cooking time will make cookies that are soft and chewy in the middle. The longer cooking time will produce crisper cookies.

1 Preheat the oven to 350°F/180°C, then grease 3 cookie sheets. Place the butter, granulated sugar, and brown sugar in a bowl and beat until light and fluffy. Gradually beat in the egg and vanilla extract.

2 Sift the flour, cocoa, and baking soda into the mixture and stir in carefully. Stir in the chocolate chips and walnuts. Drop spoonfuls of the dough onto the prepared cookie sheets, spaced well apart to allow for spreading.

3 Bake in the oven for 10–15 minutes, or until the mixture has spread and the cookies are starting to feel firm. Let cool on the cookie sheets for 2 minutes, then transfer to wire racks to cool completely.

easter cookies

makes 24   **prep: 20 mins, plus 20 mins cooling**   **cook: 10–15 mins**

In spite of their name, these cookies are good to eat at any time of year! The candied peel and currants give them a fruity, spicy taste, and a dusting of sugar makes them an especially sweet treat.

INGREDIENTS

6 oz/175 g butter, softened, plus extra for greasing

generous ¾ cup golden superfine sugar

1 egg, beaten

2 tbsp milk

¼ cup chopped candied peel

generous ⅔ cup currants

2½ cups all-purpose flour, plus extra for dusting

1 tsp allspice

GLAZE

1 egg white, lightly beaten

2 tbsp golden superfine sugar

NUTRITIONAL INFORMATION	
Calories	159
Protein	2g
Carbohydrate	25g
Sugars	14g
Fat	7g
Saturates	4g

variation

If you do not like candied peel, you can substitute another ⅓ cup of extra currants instead.

cook's tip

Be careful when sprinkling the sugar over the glaze—any sugar sprinkled directly on to the cookie sheet will burn onto its surface.

1 Preheat the oven to 350°F/180°C, then grease 2 large cookie sheets. Place the butter and sugar in a bowl and beat until light and fluffy. Gradually beat in the egg and milk. Stir in the candied peel and currants, then sift in the flour and allspice. Mix together to make a firm dough. Knead lightly until smooth.

2 On a floured counter, roll out the dough to ¼-inch/5-mm thick and use a 2-inch/5-cm round cookie cutter to stamp out the cookies. Re-roll the dough trimmings and stamp out more cookies until the dough is used up. Place the cookies on the prepared cookie sheets and bake in the preheated oven for 10 minutes.

3 Remove from the oven to glaze. Brush with the egg white and sprinkle with the superfine sugar, then return to the oven for an additional 5 minutes, or until lightly browned. Let cool on the cookie sheets for 2 minutes, then transfer to wire racks to cool completely.

mexican pastelitos

makes 40

prep: 20 mins, plus
20 mins cooling

cook: 30–40 mins

These little South American-style cookies melt in the mouth. They are traditionally served at Mexican weddings and are coated in confectioners' sugar to reflect the white of the bride's dress.

INGREDIENTS

8 oz/225 g butter, softened, plus extra for greasing
¼ cup golden superfine sugar
generous 1½ cups all-purpose flour
generous ¾ cup cornstarch
1 tsp ground cinnamon
½ cup confectioners' sugar, sifted, to decorate

NUTRITIONAL INFORMATION

Calories	.82
Protein	.1g
Carbohydrate	.10g
Sugars	.3g
Fat	.5g
Saturates	.3g

cook's tip

These cookies are traditionally made to this small size, but you could make larger cookies, if you prefer.

1 Preheat the oven to 325°F/160°C, then grease 2 cookie sheets. Place the butter and superfine sugar in a bowl and beat until light and fluffy. Sift the flour, cornstarch, and cinnamon into a separate bowl, then gradually work them into the creamed mixture with a wooden spoon. When well mixed, knead until smooth.

2 Take 1 teaspoon of the mixture at a time and roll into a ball. Place the little balls on the prepared cookie sheets. Bake in the preheated oven for 30–40 minutes, or until pale golden.

3 Place the confectioners' sugar in a shallow dish and toss the pastelitos in it while they are still warm. Let cool on wire racks.

lavender cookies

cook: 12 mins   **prep: 15 mins, plus 20 mins cooling**   **makes 12**

Guests will be surprised and delighted by these original and unusual fragrant cookies, which make the perfect accompaniment to a cup of coffee in the afternoon.

NUTRITIONAL INFORMATION

Calories	141
Protein	2g
Carbohydrate	17g
Sugars	6g
Fat	8g
Saturates	5g

INGREDIENTS

4 oz/115 g butter, softened,
plus extra for greasing
¼ cup golden superfine sugar,
plus extra for dusting
1 tsp chopped lavender leaves
finely grated rind of 1 lemon
1¼ cups all-purpose flour

cook's tip

If you do not have a food processor, you can mix the dough by hand. Knead it into a ball before rolling out in Step 2.

1 Preheat the oven to 300°F/150°C, then grease a large cookie sheet. Place the superfine sugar and lavender leaves in a food processor. Process until the lavender is very finely chopped, then add the butter and lemon rind and process until light and fluffy. Transfer to a large bowl. Sift in the flour and beat until the mixture forms a stiff dough.

2 Place the dough on a sheet of parchment paper and place another sheet on top. Gently press down with a rolling pin and roll out to ⅛–½-inch/3–5-mm thick. Remove the top sheet of paper and stamp out circles from the dough using a 2¾-inch/7-cm round cookie cutter. Re-knead and re-roll the dough trimmings and stamp out more cookies.

3 Using a spatula, carefully transfer the cookies to the prepared cookie sheet. Prick the cookies with a fork and bake in the preheated oven for 12 minutes, or until pale brown. Let cool on the cookie sheet for 2 minutes, then transfer to a wire rack to cool completely.

oat & raisin cookies

makes 10

prep: 20 mins, plus 30 mins cooling

cook: 15 mins

These oaty, fruity cookies couldn't be easier to make and are delicious with a hot drink.

INGREDIENTS

4 tbsp butter, plus extra for greasing

generous ⅝ cup superfine sugar

1 egg, beaten

scant ⅓ cup all-purpose flour

½ tsp salt

½ tsp baking powder

2 cups rolled oats

¾ cup raisins

2 tbsp sesame seeds

NUTRITIONAL INFORMATION

Calories	.227
Protein	.4g
Carbohydrate	.39g
Sugars	.22g
Fat	.7g
Saturates	.3g

cook's tip

To enjoy these cookies at their best, store them in an airtight container and eat within 1 week. Make sure that they are completely cold before storing.

1 Preheat the oven to 350°F/180°C, then lightly grease 2 cookie sheets. Beat the butter and sugar together in a large bowl until light and fluffy. Gradually add the beaten egg, beating well after each addition, until thoroughly combined. Sift the flour, salt, and baking powder into the creamed mixture and mix gently to combine. Add the rolled oats, raisins, and sesame seeds and mix together thoroughly.

2 Place spoonfuls of the cookie dough, spaced well apart on the prepared cookie sheets to allow room to expand during cooking, and flatten them slightly with the back of a spoon.

3 Bake the cookies in the preheated oven for 15 minutes. Let the cookies cool slightly on the cookie sheets, then carefully transfer the cookies to a wire rack and let cool completely before serving.

coconut oat crunch bars

cook: 30 mins

prep: 15 mins, plus 30 mins cooling

makes 16

Freshly baked, these chewy oat crunch bars are always a favorite for after-school snacks and just the thing for teatime.

NUTRITIONAL INFORMATION

Calories 269

Protein 3g

Carbohydrate 32g

Sugars 19g

Fat 16g

Saturates 10g

INGREDIENTS

7 oz/200 g butter, plus extra

for greasing

1 cup raw brown sugar

2 tbsp corn syrup

3 cups rolled oats

scant ¾ cup dry unsweetened coconut

½ cup candied cherries, chopped

cook's tip

The oat crunch bars are best stored in an airtight container and eaten within 1 week. They can also be frozen for up to 1 month. Make sure they are thawed before eating.

1 Preheat the oven to 325°F/160°C, then grease a 12 x 9-inch/ 30 x 23-cm cookie sheet.

2 Heat the butter, sugar, and syrup in a large pan over low heat until just melted. Stir in the oats, coconut, and cherries and mix until evenly combined.

3 Spread the mixture evenly onto the cookie sheet and press down with the back of a spatula to form a smooth surface.

4 Bake in the preheated oven for 30 minutes. Remove from the oven and let cool on the cookie sheet for 10 minutes. Cut the crunch bars into rectangles using a sharp knife. Carefully transfer the bars to a wire rack and let cool completely.

peanut butter cookies

makes 26　　　　**prep: 20 mins, plus 20 mins cooling**　　　　**cook: 12 mins**

These are easy cookies for children to make. All of the ingredients are mixed together in one bowl, and the cookies themselves do not require any shaping or rolling out.

INGREDIENTS

4 oz /115 g butter, softened, plus extra for greasing	½ tsp vanilla extract
	⅔ cup all-purpose flour
scant ½ cup crunchy peanut butter	½ tsp baking soda
generous ½ cup golden superfine sugar	½ tsp baking powder
generous ½ cup brown sugar	pinch of salt
1 egg, beaten	1½ cups rolled oats

NUTRITIONAL INFORMATION

Calories 125

Protein 2g

Carbohydrate 15g

Sugars 10g

Fat 7g

Saturates 3g

variation

You can use smooth peanut butter rather than crunchy peanut butter, if you prefer.

cook's tip

When you flatten the cookies with a fork, make a slight impression on the surface with the tines of the fork to give them extra texture.

1 Preheat the oven to 350°F/180°C, then grease 3 cookie sheets. Place the butter and peanut butter in a bowl and beat together. Beat in the superfine and brown sugars, then gradually beat in the egg and vanilla extract.

2 Sift the flour, baking soda, baking powder, and salt into the bowl and stir in the oats. Drop spoonfuls of the cookie dough onto the cookie sheets, spaced well apart to allow for spreading. Flatten slightly with a fork.

3 Bake in the preheated oven for 12 minutes, or until lightly browned. Let cool on the cookie sheets for 2 minutes, then transfer to wire racks to cool completely.

spiced cocktail bites

makes about 20　　　**prep: 15 mins, plus** 🕐
45 mins chilling (optional)　　　**cook: 20 mins** 🕐

*If you are looking for something a little different and original
to help a dinner party go with a swing, these spicy cookies are
ideal for serving with pre-dinner drinks.*

INGREDIENTS

4 oz/115 g butter, plus
extra for greasing

1 cup all-purpose flour,
plus extra for dusting

2 tsp curry powder

generous ¾ cup grated Cheddar cheese

2 tsp poppy seeds

1 tsp black onion seeds

1 egg yolk

cumin seeds, for sprinkling

NUTRITIONAL INFORMATION

Calories 88

Protein 2g

Carbohydrate 6g

Sugars 0g

Fat 7g

Saturates 4g

---

variation

If you prefer, sprinkle with a little
freshly ground cumin instead of
the cumin seeds.

cook's tip

Chilling the dough and the
rolled cookies helps the cookies
to maintain their shape, but if
you are short of time, it will
not matter if you do not do so.

1 Preheat the oven
to 375°F/190°C, then
grease 2 cookie sheets. Sift the
flour and curry powder into a
bowl. Cut the butter into
pieces and add to the flour.
Rub in until the mixture
resembles bread crumbs,
then stir in the cheese, poppy
seeds, and black onion seeds.
Stir in the egg yolk and mix
to a firm dough.

2 Wrap the dough in
plastic wrap and chill in
the refrigerator for 30 minutes.
On a floured counter, roll out
the dough to ⅛-inch/3-mm
thick. Stamp out shapes with
a cutter. Re-roll the trimmings
and stamp out more cookies
until the dough is used up.

3 Place the cookies on the
prepared cookie sheets
and sprinkle with the cumin
seeds. Let chill for an
additional 15 minutes. Bake
in the preheated oven for
20 minutes, or until crisp and
golden. Serve warm or transfer
to wire racks to cool.

citrus crescents

prep: 10 mins, plus 20 mins cooling

cook: 15 mins

For a sweet treat, try these attractive crescent-shaped cookies, which have a lovely citrus tang to them.

INGREDIENTS

3½ oz/100 g butter, softened, plus extra for greasing

generous ½ cup superfine sugar, plus extra for dusting (optional)

1 egg, separated

generous 1¼ cups all-purpose flour, plus extra for dusting

grated rind of 1 orange

grated rind of 1 lemon

grated rind of 1 lime

2–3 tbsp orange juice

NUTRITIONAL INFORMATION

Calories	72
Protein	. . . . .1g
Carbohydrate	. . . . .10g
Sugars	. . . . .3g
Fat	. . . . .4g
Saturates	. . . . .2g

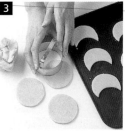

cook's tip

Store the citrus crescents in an airtight container and eat within 1 week. Alternatively, they can be frozen for up to 1 month.

1 Preheat the oven to 400°F/200°C, then lightly grease 2 cookie sheets. Beat the butter and sugar together in a large bowl until light and fluffy, then gradually beat in the egg yolk.

2 Sift the flour into the creamed mixture and mix until evenly combined.

Add the orange, lemon and lime rinds to the mixture with enough of the orange juice to form a soft dough.

3 Roll out the dough on a lightly floured counter. Stamp out circles using a 3-inch/7.5-cm cookie cutter. Make crescent shapes by cutting away a quarter of

each circle. Re-roll the trimmings to make 25 crescents, then place on the prepared cookie sheets. Prick the surface of each crescent with a fork.

4 Lightly whisk the egg white in a small bowl and brush it over the cookies. Dust with extra superfine sugar (if using), then bake in the

oven, for 12–15 minutes. Carefully transfer the cookies to a wire rack and let cool until crisp before serving.

lemon jumbles

cook: 20 mins

prep: 10 mins, plus 20 mins cooling

makes 50

These lemony, melt-in-the-mouth cookies are made extra special by dredging with confectioners' sugar just before serving.

NUTRITIONAL INFORMATION

Calories 50

Protein 1g

Carbohydrate 8g

Sugars 3g

Fat 2g

Saturates 1g

INGREDIENTS

3½ oz/100 g butter, softened, plus extra for greasing

⅔ cup superfine sugar

grated rind of 1 lemon

1 egg, beaten

4 tbsp lemon juice

2¼ cups all-purpose flour, plus extra for dusting

1 tsp baking powder

1 tbsp milk

confectioners' sugar, for dredging

variation

If you prefer, shape the dough into other shapes—letters of the alphabet or geometric shapes—or just make into round cookies.

1 Preheat the oven to 325°F/160°C, then lightly grease several cookie sheets. Beat the butter, superfine sugar and lemon rind together in a large bowl until pale and fluffy. Add the beaten egg and lemon juice, a little at a time, beating well after each addition.

2 Sift the flour and baking powder into the creamed mixture and blend together. Add the milk, mixing to form a soft dough.

3 Turn the dough out onto a lightly floured counter and divide into 50 equal-size pieces.

4 Roll each piece into a sausage shape with your hands and twist in the center to make an "S" shape. Place on the cookie sheets and bake in the oven for 15–20 minutes. Transfer to a wire rack and let cool completely. Dredge with confectioners' sugar to serve.

pesto palmiers

makes 20 **prep: 10 mins, plus** ⏲ **20 mins chilling** **cook: 10 mins** ⏲

Serve these flaky and light palmiers to nibble with drinks, or as an accompaniment to a hearty, warming soup.

INGREDIENTS

butter, for greasing

all-purpose flour, for dusting

9 oz/250 g ready-made puff pastry

3 tbsp green or red pesto

1 egg yolk, beaten with 1 tbsp water

¼ cup freshly grated Parmesan cheese

NUTRITIONAL INFORMATION

Calories	70
Protein	. . . . .2g
Carbohydrate	. . . . .5g
Sugars	. . . . .0g
Fat	. . . . .5g
Saturates	. . . . .1g

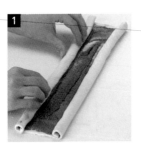

variation

As an alternative to the pesto filling, substitute prosciutto or chopped anchovy fillets.

1 Preheat the oven to 400°F/200°C, then grease a cookie sheet. On a floured counter, roll out the pastry to a 14 x 6-inch/ 35 x 15-cm rectangle and trim the edges with a sharp knife. Spread the pesto evenly over the pastry. Roll up the ends tightly to meet in the center of the pastry.

2 Wrap in plastic wrap and chill in the refrigerator for 20 minutes, until firm, then remove from the refrigerator and unwrap. Brush with the beaten egg yolk on all sides. Cut across into ½-inch/1-cm thick slices. Place the slices on the prepared cookie sheet.

3 Bake in the preheated oven for 10 minutes, or until crisp and golden. Remove from the oven and immediately sprinkle over the Parmesan cheese. Serve the palmiers warm or transfer to a wire rack and let cool to room temperature.

cheese & rosemary sables

⏲ **cook: 10 mins**   ⏱ **prep: 15 mins, plus 30 mins chilling**   **makes 40**

The dough for these biscuits is made in a food processor, making these sables a quick and easy savory treat.

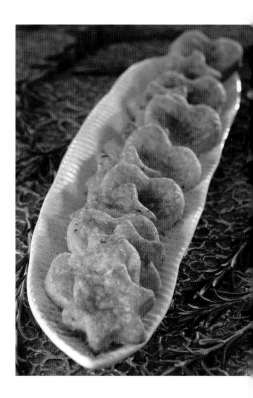

NUTRITIONAL INFORMATION

Calories	.80
Protein	.2g
Carbohydrate	.5g
Sugars	.0g
Fat	.6g
Saturates	.4g

INGREDIENTS

8 oz/225 g cold butter, diced, plus extra for greasing

1¾ cups all-purpose flour

2½ cups grated Gruyère cheese

½ tsp cayenne pepper

2 tsp finely chopped fresh rosemary leaves

1 egg yolk, beaten with 1 tbsp water

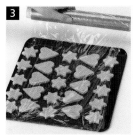

1 Preheat the oven to 350°F/180°C, then grease 2 cookie sheets. Place the flour, butter, cheese, cayenne pepper, and rosemary in a food processor. Pulse until the mixture forms a dough, adding a little cold water, if necessary, to bring the mixture together.

2 On a floured counter, roll out the dough to ¼-inch/5-mm thick. Stamp out shapes such as stars and hearts with 2½-inch/6-cm cutters.

3 Place the shapes on the prepared cookie sheets, then cover with plastic wrap and let chill in the refrigerator for 30 minutes, or until firm. Brush with the beaten egg yolk and bake in the oven for 10 minutes, or until golden brown. Let cool on the cookie sheets for 2 minutes, then serve warm or transfer to wire racks to cool.

cook's tip

If you do not have a food processor, then place all the ingredients in a large mixing bowl and mix them together by hand.

cheese straws

makes 24

20 mins, plus 30 mins chilling

cook: 10–15 mins

Crisp cheese straws are irresistibly moreish. They make a wonderful party food, and are popular with children and adults alike.

INGREDIENTS

generous ¾ cup all-purpose flour, plus extra for dusting

pinch of salt

1 tsp curry powder

2 oz/55 g butter, plus extra for greasing

½ cup grated Cheddar cheese

1 egg, beaten

poppy and cumin seeds, for sprinkling

variation

The same dough can be cut into cookie shapes rather than straws, if you prefer.

cook's tip

Make sure that you mix the dough thoroughly to prevent any cracks in the dough straws, otherwise they may split apart while cooking.

1 Sift the flour, salt, and curry powder into a bowl. Add the butter and rub in until the mixture resembles bread crumbs. Add the cheese and half the egg and mix to form a dough. Wrap in plastic wrap and chill in the refrigerator for 30 minutes.

2 Preheat the oven to 400°F/200°C, then grease several cookie sheets. On a floured counter, roll out the dough to ¼-inch/5-mm thick. Cut into 3 x ½-inch/ 7.5 x 1-cm strips. Pinch the strips lightly along the sides and place on the prepared cookie sheets.

3 Brush the straws with the remaining egg and sprinkle half with poppy seeds and half with cumin seeds. Bake in the preheated oven for 10–15 minutes, or until golden. Transfer to wire racks to cool.

breads & buns

There are few cooking processes that are as satisfying as bread-making. It is not just the special flavor of homemade bread, or the mouthwatering aroma in the kitchen as it cooks, but there is something magical about seeing an unprepossessing lump of dough turning into a perfect loaf. When you taste your own bread, you will be taken back to those days when there was a family baker on every High Street.

If you think that bread-making is a difficult and lengthy process, the recipes in this section will convince you otherwise. With active dry yeast, it could not be easier to make yeast doughs, and although it does take time for a dough to rise, you can be getting on with other things while that is happening.

A basic bread dough can provide the basis of a hot Pepperoni Pizza (see page 54), and with the addition of a few other simple ingredients, can be transformed into a wide variety of delicious sweet and savory loaves and buns, such as Cheese & Chive Braid (see page 57), Apricot & Walnut Bread (see page 84), or Chelsea Buns (see page 82). There are recipes for traditional festive breads, such as Stollen (see page 74) or Hot Cross Buns (see page 78). There are also recipes in this section for yeast-free teabreads, such as Date & Walnut Teabread (see page 89) or Banana & Chocolate Chip Loaf (see page 94), which are perfect for slicing and buttering, and a classic Irish Soda Bread (see page 60) that takes minutes to make.

sun-dried tomato rolls

serves 8

prep: 15 mins, plus 2 hrs rising/cooling

cook: 15 mins

These white rolls have the addition of finely chopped sun-dried tomatoes. The tomatoes are available at most supermarkets.

INGREDIENTS

3½ oz/100 g butter, melted and cooled slightly, plus extra for greasing

1½ cups strong white bread flour, plus extra for dusting

½ tsp salt

¼-oz/7-g envelope active dry yeast

3 tbsp milk, warmed, plus extra for brushing

2 eggs, beaten

1¾ oz/50 g sun-dried tomatoes, well drained and finely chopped

NUTRITIONAL INFORMATION

Calories	.214
Protein	.5g
Carbohydrate	.22g
Sugars	.1g
Fat	.12g
Saturates	.7g

variation

Add some finely chopped anchovies or olives to the dough in Step 5 for extra flavour, if you like.

1 Lightly grease a baking tray. Sift the flour and salt into a large bowl. Stir in the yeast, then pour in the butter, milk, and eggs. Mix together to form a dough.

2 Turn the dough onto a floured counter and knead for 5 minutes. Alternatively, use an electric mixer with a dough hook.

3 Place the dough in a greased bowl, cover, and let rise in a warm place for 1–1½ hours, or until doubled in size. Punch down the dough for 2–3 minutes.

4 Preheat the oven to 450°F/230°C. Knead the sun-dried tomatoes into the dough, sprinkling the counter with a little extra flour because the tomatoes are quite oily. Divide the dough into 8 equal-size balls and place them on the cookie sheet. Cover and let stand for 30 minutes, or until doubled in size.

5 Brush the rolls with milk and bake in the oven for 10–15 minutes, or until golden brown. Transfer the rolls to a wire rack and let cool slightly before serving.

mini focaccia

cook: 25 mins

prep: 15 mins, plus 2 hrs rising/cooling

serves 4

This is a delicious Italian bread made with olive oil. The topping of red onions and thyme is particularly flavorsome.

NUTRITIONAL INFORMATION

Calories 439

Protein 9g

Carbohydrate 71g

Sugars 3g

Fat 15g

Saturates 2g

INGREDIENTS

2 tbsp olive oil, plus extra for oiling

2¼ cups strong white flour, plus extra for dusting

½ tsp salt

¼-oz/7-g envelope active dry yeast

scant 1¼ cups lukewarm water

generous ½ cup pitted green or black olives, halved

TOPPING

2 red onions, sliced

2 tbsp olive oil

1 tsp sea salt

1 tbsp thyme leaves

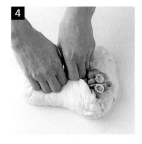

variation

Use this quantity of dough to make 1 large focaccia, if you prefer.

1 Oil a cookie sheet. Sift the flour and salt into a large bowl. Stir in the yeast, pour in the oil and water and mix to form a dough.

2 Turn the dough out onto a floured counter and knead for 5 minutes. Alternatively, use an electric mixer with a dough hook.

3 Place the dough in an oiled bowl, cover, and let stand in a warm place for 1–1½ hours, or until doubled in size. Punch down the dough by kneading it again for 1–2 minutes.

4 Knead half of the olives into the dough. Divide the dough into quarters and shape the quarters into circles.

Place them on the cookie sheet and push your fingers into the dough to create a dimpled effect.

5 To make the topping, sprinkle the red onions and remaining olives over the circles. Drizzle the oil over the top and sprinkle with the sea salt and thyme leaves. Cover and let stand for 30 minutes.

6 Preheat the oven to 375°F/190°C, then bake for 20–25 minutes, or until the focaccia are golden. Transfer to a wire rack and let cool before serving.

pepperoni pizza

serves 2   **prep: 20 mins, plus 30 mins rising**   **cook: 14–20 mins**

Pepperoni and tomato complement one another perfectly on this filling pizza. Dried red chili flakes give the topping quite a kick!

INGREDIENTS

PIZZA DOUGH

generous 1½ cups strong white bread flour, plus extra for dusting

2 tsp active dry yeast

1 tsp golden superfine sugar

½ tsp salt

1 tbsp olive oil, plus extra for brushing

¾ cup tepid water

TOPPING

1¾ cups canned chopped tomatoes, drained

2 garlic cloves, crushed

1 tsp dried oregano

1–2 tsp dried chili flakes

8 oz/225 g pepperoni, sliced

2 tbsp drained capers

8 oz/225 g mozzarella cheese, cut into thin slices

NUTRITIONAL INFORMATION

Calories 1154

Protein 65g

Carbohydrate 97g

Sugars 12g

Fat 59g

Saturates 25g

variation

If you would prefer a pizza with a little less heat, you can omit the chili flakes from the topping.

cook's tip

To save time, you can use a pizza dough mix, which can be found in any large food store. These make a crisper dough than ready-made versions.

1 Sift the flour into a warmed bowl. Stir in the yeast, sugar, and salt and make a well in the center. Stir the olive oil into the water, then stir into the flour. Mix to form a soft dough. Knead the dough on a lightly floured counter for 5–10 minutes, or until it becomes smooth and elastic. Transfer the dough to a clean, warmed, oiled bowl and cover with plastic wrap. Let stand in a warm place for 30 minutes, or until the dough has doubled in size.

2 Preheat the oven to 425°F/220°C, then brush 2 cookie sheets with oil. Turn the dough out onto a lightly floured counter and knead lightly for 1 minute.

Divide it in half and roll out each piece into a 10-inch/ 25-cm circle. Place on the prepared cookie sheets.

3 To make the topping, place the drained tomatoes, garlic, and oregano in a bowl and stir to mix. Spread half the mixture over each dough circle, leaving a margin round the edges.

4 Bake in the preheated oven for 7–10 minutes, or until the rim on each pizza is pale golden. Scatter the chili flakes over the pizzas, then arrange the pepperoni slices and capers on top. Finally, place the mozzarella cheese slices on top. Return the pizzas to the oven for an additional 7–10 minutes, then serve immediately.

black olive focaccia

serves 12   **prep: 20–25 mins, plus 2 hrs rising**   **cook: 30–35 mins**

Focaccia is an Italian flatbread made with olive oil. Try serving it with soups or salads, or on its own as an indulgent snack.

INGREDIENTS

scant 4 cups strong white bread flour, plus extra for dusting

1 tsp salt

2 tsp active dry yeast

1½ cups tepid water

6 tbsp extra virgin olive oil, plus extra for brushing

⅔ cup pitted black olives, coarsely chopped

1 tsp rock salt

NUTRITIONAL INFORMATION

Calories	200
Protein	5g
Carbohydrate	31g
Sugars	1g
Fat	7g
Saturates	1g

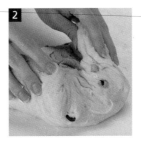

cook's tip

As the flavor of the olive oil is the most important part of this bread recipe, try to use a good-quality, well-flavored olive oil.

1 Sift the flour and salt into a warmed bowl and stir in the yeast. Pour in the water and 2 tablespoons of the olive oil and mix to a soft dough. Knead the dough on a lightly floured counter for 5–10 minutes, or until it becomes smooth and elastic. Transfer it to a clean, warmed, oiled bowl and cover with plastic wrap. Let stand in a warm place for 1 hour, or until the dough has doubled in size.

2 Brush 2 cookie sheets with oil. Punch the dough to knock out the air, then knead on a lightly floured counter for 1 minute. Add the olives and knead until combined. Divide the dough in half and shape into 2 ovals 11 x 9-inches/28 x 23-cm long, and place on the prepared cookie sheets. Cover with oiled plastic wrap and let stand in a warm place for 1 hour, or until the dough is puffy.

3 Preheat the oven to 400°F/200°C. Press your fingers into the dough to make dimples, drizzle over 2 tablespoons of oil, and sprinkle with the rock salt.

Bake in the preheated oven for 30–35 minutes, or until golden. Drizzle with the remaining olive oil and cover with a cloth, to give a soft crust. Slice each loaf into 6 pieces and serve warm.

cheese & chive braid

cook: 35 mins

prep: 30 mins, plus 1 hr 45 mins rising

serves 10

This delicious, flavored bread is ideal for serving with soup or as an accompaniment to a ploughman's lunch.

NUTRITIONAL INFORMATION

Calories 237

Protein 9g

Carbohydrate 35g

Sugars 2g

Fat 8g

Saturates 4g

INGREDIENTS

3½ cups strong white bread flour, plus extra for dusting

1 tsp salt

1 tsp superfine sugar

1½ tsp active dry yeast

2 tbsp butter

generous 1 cup coarsely grated Cheddar cheese

3 tbsp snipped fresh chives

4 scallions, chopped

⅔ cup tepid milk

¾ cup tepid water

vegetable oil, for brushing

beaten egg, for glazing

variation

This dough could be used to make small rolls instead of one large loaf.

1 Sift the flour and salt into a warmed bowl and stir in the sugar and yeast. Rub in the butter, then stir in the cheese, chives, and scallions. Make a well in the center. Mix together the milk and water and pour into the well. Mix to make a soft dough. Turn the dough out onto a lightly floured counter and knead for

10 minutes, or until it is smooth and elastic.

2 Transfer the dough to a clean, oiled bowl and cover with plastic wrap. Let stand in a warm place for 1 hour, or until doubled in size. Preheat the oven to 425°F/220°C, then brush a large cookie sheet with oil. Turn the dough out onto a floured

counter and knead for 1 minute. Divide the dough into 3 pieces. Roll out each piece into a rope shape and braid the 3 pieces together, pinching the ends to seal.

3 Place on the prepared cookie sheet and cover with oiled plastic wrap. Let stand in a warm place for 45 minutes, or until doubled in

size. Brush with beaten egg and bake in the preheated oven for 20 minutes.

4 Reduce the oven temperature to 350°F/180°C and bake for an additional 15 minutes, or until golden brown and the loaf sounds hollow when tapped on the bottom. Serve warm or cold.

citrus bread

cook: 35 mins

prep: 25 mins, plus 2 hrs rising/cooling

makes 1 loaf

variation

Use a flavored honey, such as orange blossom or pine to glaze the bread, if you like.

This sweet loaf is flavored with citrus fruits. As with Tropical Fruit Bread (see page 66), it is excellent served at breakfast.

INGREDIENTS

4 tbsp butter, cut into small pieces, plus extra for greasing

3 cups strong white bread flour, plus extra for dusting

½ tsp salt

¼ cup superfine sugar

¼-oz/7-g envelope active dry yeast

5–6 tbsp orange juice

4 tbsp lemon juice

3–4 tbsp lime juice

⅔ cup lukewarm water

1 orange

1 lemon

1 lime

2 tbsp honey

cook's tip

It is important to use lukewarm water when using active dry yeast because this encourages fermentation. Active dry yeast is available from most large supermarkets and health food stores.

1 Lightly grease a cookie sheet with a little butter. Sift the flour and salt into a large bowl. Stir in the sugar and yeast. Add the butter and rub it into the mixture using your fingertips. Add the orange, lemon and lime juice, and the water and mix to form a dough.

2 Place the dough on a lightly floured counter and knead for 5 minutes. Alternatively, use an electric mixer with a dough hook. Place the dough in a greased bowl, cover, and let rise in a warm place for 1 hour, or until it has doubled in size.

3 Grate the rind of the orange, lemon, and lime, then knead the fruit rinds into the dough.

4 Divide the dough into 2 balls, making one slightly bigger than the other. Place the larger ball on the prepared cookie sheet and set the smaller one on top. Push a floured finger through the center of the dough. Cover and let stand for an additional 40 minutes, or until springy to the touch.

5 Preheat the oven to 425°F/220°C, then bake the bread for 35 minutes. Remove from the oven and transfer to a wire rack to cool. Glaze with the honey.

irish soda bread

serves 12 | **prep: 10 mins** | **cook: 35–40 mins**

Soda bread contains no yeast, so it is quick and easy to make—ideal when you're expecting guests for a meal.

INGREDIENTS

2 cups white all-purpose flour,
plus extra for dusting

2 cups whole-wheat flour

1½ tsp baking soda

1 tsp salt

1 tsp brown sugar

generous 1¾ cups buttermilk

NUTRITIONAL INFORMATION

Calories 167

Protein 6g

Carbohydrate 35g

Sugars 3g

Fat 1g

Saturates 0g

cook's tip

Buttermilk is usually available in most large food stores, but if you cannot find it, you can substitute ordinary milk instead.

1 Preheat the oven to 450°F/230°C, then dust a cookie sheet with flour. Sift the white flour, whole-wheat flour, baking soda, and salt into a bowl and stir in the sugar. Make a well in the center and pour in enough of the buttermilk to make a dough that is soft but not too wet and sticky. Add a little more buttermilk, if necessary.

2 Turn the dough out onto a floured counter and knead very briefly into a large circle, 2-inches/5-cm thick. Dust lightly with flour and, using a sharp knife, mark the top of the loaf with a deep cross.

3 Place the loaf on the cookie sheet and bake in the preheated oven for 15 minutes. Reduce the oven temperature to 400°F/200°C and bake for an additional 20–25 minutes, or until the loaf sounds hollow when tapped on the bottom. Transfer to a wire rack to cool, and eat while still warm.

chile cheese cornbread

cook: 20 mins   **prep: 10 mins, plus 20 mins cooling**   serves 8

This golden yellow bread spiked with chiles was originally cooked over an open fire by pioneer settlers.

NUTRITIONAL INFORMATION

Calories 409

Protein 15g

Carbohydrate 43g

Sugars 3g

Fat 20g

Saturates 11g

INGREDIENTS

2 oz/55 g butter, melted, plus

extra for greasing

generous ¾ cup self-rising flour

1 tbsp baking powder

1 tsp salt

1½ cups fine cornmeal

1½ cups grated mature Cheddar cheese

2 eggs, beaten

1¼ cups milk

1 fresh red chile, seeded and

finely chopped

cook's tip

This delicious chile cornbread loses its freshness fairly quickly, so it is best eaten on the day that it is made.

1 Preheat the oven to 400°F/200°C. Grease a heavy-bottom 9-inch/23-cm cake pan or ovenproof skillet and line the bottom with waxed paper. Sift the flour, baking powder, and salt into a bowl, then stir in the cornmeal and a generous cup of the grated Cheddar cheese.

2 Pour the melted butter into a bowl and stir in the eggs and milk. Pour onto the dry ingredients, add the chile, then mix quickly until just combined. Do not overmix.

3 Spoon the mixture into the prepared pan, scatter the remaining cheese on top, and bake in the preheated oven for 20 minutes, or until risen and golden. Let cool in the pan for 2 minutes, then turn out onto a wire rack to cool completely.

cheese & ham loaf

serves 6   **prep: 25 mins, plus** ⏲ **30 mins cooling**   **cook: 1 hr** ⏲

This recipe is a quick way to make tasty bread, using self-rising flour and baking powder to ensure a good rising.

INGREDIENTS

2¾ oz/75 g butter, cut into small pieces, plus extra for greasing

1½ cups self-rising flour

1 tsp salt

2 tsp baking powder

1 tsp paprika

1⅛ cups sharp cheese, grated

2¾ oz/75 g smoked ham, chopped

2 eggs, beaten

⅔ cup milk

NUTRITIONAL INFORMATION

Calories 360

Protein 14g

Carbohydrate 31g

Sugars 2g

Fat 21g

Saturates 13g

cook's tip

This tasty bread is best eaten on the day it is made as it does not keep for very long. Let cool completely before serving.

1 Preheat the oven to 350°F/180°C. Grease a 1-lb/450-g loaf pan with butter and line the bottom with parchment paper.

2 Sift the flour, salt, baking powder, and paprika into a large bowl. Add the butter and rub it in with your fingertips until the mixture resembles fine bread crumbs. Stir in the cheese and ham. Add the beaten eggs and milk to the dry ingredients in the bowl and combine well, then spoon into the prepared loaf pan.

3 Bake in the preheated oven for 1 hour, or until the loaf is well risen. Let the bread cool in the pan for 10 minutes, then turn out and transfer to a wire rack to cool completely. Serve the bread cut into thick slices.

cheesy bread

cook: 30 mins

prep: 25 mins, plus 30 mins cooling

serves 8

This is a quick bread to make. To enjoy it at its best, it should be eaten as fresh as possible.

NUTRITIONAL INFORMATION

Calories	190
Protein	7g
Carbohydrate	22g
Sugars	1g
Fat	9g
Saturates	5g

INGREDIENTS

2 tbsp butter, melted, plus extra
for greasing

1½ cups self-rising flour

1 tsp salt

1 tsp mustard powder

⅞ cup sharp cheese, grated

2 tbsp snipped fresh chives

1 egg, beaten

⅔ cup milk

cook's tip

You can use any hard sharp cheese of your choice for this recipe, such as Cheddar, Cheshire, or Jack cheese.

1 Preheat the oven to 375°F/190°C. Grease a 9-inch/23-cm square cake pan with a little butter and line the bottom with parchment paper.

2 Sift the flour, salt, and mustard powder into a large bowl. Set aside 3 tablespoons of the grated sharp cheese for sprinkling, then stir the remaining grated cheese into the bowl, together with the snipped chives. Mix together well. Add the beaten egg, melted butter, and milk to the dry ingredients and stir thoroughly to combine.

3 Pour into the prepared pan and spread with a knife. Sprinkle over the reserved grated cheese.

4 Bake in the preheated oven for 30 minutes. Let the bread cool slightly in the pan. Turn out onto a wire rack to cool completely. Cut into triangles to serve.

mango twist bread

cook: 30 mins

prep: 15 mins, plus 2 hrs 40 mins rising/cooling

makes 1 loaf

This is a sweet bread which has puréed mango mixed into the dough, resulting in a moist loaf with an exotic flavor.

NUTRITIONAL INFORMATION

Calories 228

Protein 6g

Carbohydrate 46g

Sugars 18g

Fat 4g

Saturates 2g

INGREDIENTS

3 tbsp butter, cut into small pieces, plus extra for greasing

3 cups strong white bread flour, plus extra for dusting

1 tsp salt

¼-oz/7-g envelope active dry yeast

1 tsp ground ginger

¼ cup firmly packed brown sugar

1 small mango, peeled, seeded, and puréed

scant 1¼ cups lukewarm water

2 tbsp honey

⅔ cup golden raisins

1 egg, beaten

confectioners' sugar, for dusting

variation

Substitute the golden raisins with the same amount of raisins and replace the ground ginger with ground cinnamon, if you prefer.

cook's tip

You can tell when the bread is cooked as it will sound hollow when tapped on the bottom. If it sounds heavy, then return to the oven for an additional 5 minutes.

1 Grease a cookie sheet with a little butter. Sift the flour and salt into a large bowl, stir in the yeast, ground ginger, and brown sugar. Rub in the butter with your fingertips.

2 Stir in the mango purée, water, and honey and mix together to form a dough.

3 Place the dough on a lightly floured counter and knead for 5 minutes, or until smooth. Alternatively, use an electric mixer with a dough hook. Place the dough in a greased bowl, cover, and let stand to rise in a warm place for 1 hour, or until it has doubled in size.

4 Knead in the golden raisins and shape the dough into 2 sausage shapes, each 10-inches/25-cm long. Carefully twist the 2 pieces together and pinch the ends to seal. Place the dough on the cookie sheet, cover, and let stand in a warm place for an additional 40 minutes.

5 Preheat the oven to 425°F/220°C. Brush the loaf with the egg and bake in the oven for 30 minutes, or until golden brown. Let cool on a wire rack. Dust with confectioners' sugar before serving.

tropical fruit bread

makes 1 loaf   **prep: 15 mins, plus 1 hr ⏱ 40 mins rising/cooling**   **cook: 30 mins ⏱**

The exotic flavors of pineapple and mango in this bread will bring a touch of sunshine to your breakfast table.

INGREDIENTS

2 tbsp butter, cut into small pieces, plus extra for greasing

2¼ cups strong white bread flour, plus extra for dusting

⅞ cup bran

½ tsp salt

½ tsp ground ginger

¼-oz/7-g envelope active dry yeast

2 tbsp brown sugar

scant 1¼ cups tepid water

½ cup candied pineapple, finely chopped

1 oz/25 g dried mango, finely chopped

generous ⅓ cup dry unsweetened coconut, toasted

1 egg, beaten

2 tbsp coconut shreds

variation

Replace the mango with other dried fruits, such as no-soak dried apricots or dates, if you prefer.

cook's tip

To test the bread after the second rising, gently poke the dough with your finger—it should spring back if it has risen enough.

1 Grease a cookie sheet. Sift the flour into a large bowl. Stir in the bran, salt, ginger, yeast, and sugar. Add the butter and rub it in with your fingertips, then add the water and mix to form a dough.

2 Knead the dough on a lightly floured counter for 5–8 minutes, or until smooth. Alternatively, use an electric mixer with a dough hook. Place in a greased bowl, cover, and let rise in a warm place for 30 minutes, or until doubled in size.

3 Knead the pineapple, mango, and dry unsweetened coconut into the dough. Form into a circle and place on the cookie sheet.

Score the top with the back of a knife. Cover and let stand for an additional 30 minutes in a warm place.

4 Preheat the oven to 425°F/220°C. Brush the loaf with the egg and sprinkle with the coconut. Bake in the oven for 30 minutes, or until golden. Let cool on a wire rack before serving.

chocolate bread

makes 1 loaf

**prep: 20 mins, plus
2 hrs rising/cooling**

cook: 30 mins

*For the chocoholics among us, this bread is not only great fun
to make, but it is also even better to eat.*

INGREDIENTS

butter, for greasing

3 cups strong white bread flour, plus
extra for dusting

generous ¼ cup unsweetened cocoa

1 tsp salt

¼-oz/7-g envelope active dry yeast

2 tbsp brown sugar

1 tbsp corn oil

1¼ cups lukewarm water

butter, to serve

NUTRITIONAL INFORMATION

Calories	.228
Protein	.8g
Carbohydrate	.46g
Sugars	.4g
Fat	.3g
Saturates	.1g

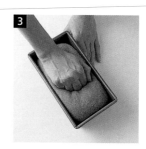

cook's tip

Before kneading the dough
on the counter, always flour it
beforehand because this
prevents the bread sticking to
the surface. However, do
not use too much flour.

1 Lightly grease a
2-lb/900-g loaf pan
with a little butter. Sift the
flour and cocoa into a large
bowl. Stir in the salt, yeast,
and brown sugar. Pour
in the oil and water and mix
together to form a dough.

2 Knead the dough on
a lightly floured counter
for 5 minutes. Alternatively,

use an electric mixer with a
dough hook. Place the dough
in a greased bowl, cover, and
let rise in a warm place for
1 hour, or until doubled in size.

3 Punch down the dough
and shape it into a loaf.
Place the dough in the pan,
cover, and let stand in a
warm place for an additional
30 minutes.

4 Preheat the oven to
400°F/200°C then bake
the bread for 25–30 minutes,
or until a hollow sound is
heard when the bottom of the
bread is tapped. Transfer the
bread to a wire rack and let
cool completely. Cut into slices
to serve with butter.

olive oil, fruit & nut cake

cook: 45 mins　　　**prep: 10 mins, plus 40 mins cooling**　　　**serves 8**

It is worth using a good-quality olive oil for this cake as this will determine its flavor. The cake will keep well in an airtight container.

NUTRITIONAL INFORMATION	
Calories	309
Protein	4g
Carbohydrate	38g
Sugars	17g
Fat	17g
Saturates	3g

INGREDIENTS

butter, for greasing

1½ cups self-rising flour

¼ cup superfine sugar

½ cup milk

4 tbsp orange juice

⅔ cup olive oil

generous ½ cup mixed dry fruit

2 tbsp pine nuts

cook's tip

Pine nuts are best known as the flavoring ingredient in the classic Italian pesto, but here they give a delicate, slightly resinous flavor to this cake.

1 Preheat the oven to 350°F/180°C. Grease a 7-inch/18-cm cake pan and line with parchment paper.

2 Sift the flour into a large bowl and stir in the superfine sugar. Make a well in the center of the dry ingredients and pour in the milk and orange juice. Stir the mixture with a wooden spoon, gradually beating in the flour and sugar. Pour in the olive oil, stirring well so that all of the ingredients are thoroughly mixed together.

3 Stir the mixed dry fruit and pine nuts into the mixture and spoon into the prepared pan. Smooth the top with a spatula.

4 Bake in the preheated oven for 45 minutes, or until the cake is golden and firm to the touch.

5 Let the cake cool in the pan for a few minutes before transferring to a wire rack to cool completely. Serve the cake warm or cold and cut into slices.

crispy-topped fruit bake

⏱ **cook: 1 hr**　　　🕐 **prep: 15 mins, plus 40 mins cooling**　　　**serves 10**

The sugar cubes give a lovely crunchy taste to this easy-to-make cake, which, served with cream, makes a splendid dessert.

variation

Replace the ground cinnamon with the same amount of allspice and use white sugar cubes instead of brown.

INGREDIENTS

butter, for greasing

12 oz/350 g cooking apples

3 tbsp lemon juice

scant 2 cups whole-wheat self-rising flour

½ tsp baking powder

1 tsp ground cinnamon, plus extra for dusting

generous 1 cup prepared blackberries, thawed if frozen, plus extra to decorate

generous ¾ cup firmly packed light brown sugar

1 egg, beaten

scant 1 cup lowfat mascarpone cheese

¼ cup brown sugar cubes, lightly crushed

sliced eating apple, to decorate

cook's tip

Try replacing the blackberries with blueberries. Use canned or frozen blueberries if the fresh fruit is unavailable.

1 Preheat the oven to 375°F/190°C. Grease and line a 2-lb/900-g loaf pan. Core, peel, and finely dice the apples. Place them in a large, heavy-bottom pan with the lemon juice, then bring to a boil, cover, and let simmer gently for 10 minutes, or until soft and pulpy. Beat thoroughly and let cool.

2 Sift the flour, baking powder, and 1 teaspoon of cinnamon into a large bowl, adding any bran that remains in the strainer. Stir in scant ¾ cup blackberries and the sugar.

3 Make a well in the center of the ingredients and add the egg, mascarpone cheese, and cooled apple purée. Mix well. Spoon the cake batter into the loaf pan and smooth the top. Sprinkle with the remaining blackberries, pressing them down into the cake batter, and top with the crushed sugar cubes.

4 Bake in the oven, for 40–45 minutes, or until golden. Let cool in the pan.

5 Remove the cake from the pan and peel away the lining paper. Serve dusted with cinnamon and decorated with extra blackberries and apple slices.

fruit loaf with apple spread

serves 4 **prep: 20 mins. plus 1 hr soaking/cooling** **cook: 2 hrs**

This sweet, fruity loaf is ideal served for tea or as a healthy snack.
The fruit spread can be made quickly while the cake is in the oven.

INGREDIENTS

butter, for greasing

2 cups rolled oats

½ cup firmly packed light brown sugar

1 tsp ground cinnamon

¾ cup golden raisins

1 cup seedless raisins

2 tbsp malt extract

1¼ cups unsweetened apple juice

1⅛ cups whole-wheat self-rising flour

1½ tsp baking powder

FRUIT SPREAD

1½ cups strawberries, washed
and hulled

2 eating apples, cored, chopped, and
mixed with 1 tbsp lemon juice to
prevent them browning

1¼ cups unsweetened apple juice

TO SERVE

strawberries

apple wedges

NUTRITIONAL INFORMATION

Calories	.733
Protein	.12g
Carbohydrate	.171g
Sugars	.110g
Fat	.5g
Saturates	.1g

variation

Substitute the strawberries in the fruit spread with other fruit, such as raspberries or blackberries.

1 Preheat the oven to 350°F/180°C. Grease and line a 2-lb/900-g loaf pan. Place the rolled oats, sugar, cinnamon, golden raisins, raisins, and malt extract in a large bowl. Pour in the apple juice, stir well, and let soak for 30 minutes.

2 Sift in the flour and baking powder, adding

any bran that remains in the strainer, and fold in using a metal spoon.

3 Spoon the into the prepared pan and bake in the oven, for 1½ hours, until firm or until a skewer inserted into the center comes out clean. Let cool in the pan for 10 minutes, then turn out onto a wire rack to cool completely.

4 Meanwhile, make the fruit spread. Place the strawberries and apples in a pan and pour in the apple juice. Bring to a boil over low heat, cover, and let simmer gently for 30 minutes. Beat the sauce well and spoon into a sterilized warmed jar. Let cool, then seal and label.

cook's tip

Make sure the jar for the spread is not too large because once opened the spread will have to be used quickly. Store the fruit spread in the refrigerator.

5 Serve the loaf, cut into slices with 1–2 tablespoons of the fruit spread and an assortment of strawberries and apple wedges.

stollen

serves 10 **prep: 30 mins, plus 5 hrs rising** **cook: 40 mins**

Stollen is a delicious spiced Austrian fruit bread with a marzipan filling and is traditionally served at Christmas.

INGREDIENTS

generous ½ cup currants

⅓ cup raisins

2 tbsp chopped candied peel

¼ cup candied cherries, rinsed, dried, and quartered

2 tbsp rum

2 oz/55 g butter

¾ cup milk

2 tbsp golden superfine sugar

generous 2¾ cups strong white bread flour, plus extra for dusting

½ tsp ground nutmeg

½ tsp ground cinnamon

seeds from 3 cardamoms

2 tsp active dry yeast

finely grated rind of 1 lemon

1 egg, beaten

scant ½ cup slivered almonds

vegetable oil, for brushing

6 oz/175 g marzipan

melted butter, for brushing

sifted confectioners' sugar, for dredging

variation

You can substitute ground allspice for the nutmeg and cinnamon, and chopped no-soak dried apricots for the cherries, if you prefer.

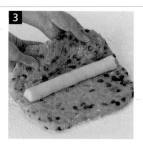

cook's tip

An enriched dough such as this takes longer to rise than ordinary bread dough, so do not be tempted to put it somewhere hot to try to speed up the process.

1 Place the currants, raisins, peel, and cherries in a bowl, stir in the rum and set aside. Place the butter, milk, and sugar in a pan over low heat and stir until the sugar dissolves and the butter melts. Cool until lukewarm. Sift the flour, nutmeg, and cinnamon into a bowl. Crush the cardamom seeds and add them. Stir in the yeast. Make a well in the center, stir in the milk mixture, lemon rind, and egg and beat into a dough.

2 Turn the dough out onto a floured counter. Knead for 5 minutes, adding more flour if necessary. Knead in the soaked fruit and the almonds. Transfer to a clean, oiled bowl. Cover with plastic wrap and let stand in a warm place for up to 3 hours, or until doubled in size. Turn out onto a floured counter, knead for 1–2 minutes, then roll out to a 10-inch/25-cm square.

3 Roll the marzipan into a sausage shorter than the length of the dough. Place in the center. Fold the dough over the marzipan, overlapping it. Seal the ends. Place seam-side down on a greased cookie sheet, cover with oiled plastic wrap, and let stand in a warm place for up to 2 hours, or until doubled in size. Preheat the oven to 375°F/190°C. Bake for 40 minutes, or until golden and hollow sounding when tapped. Brush with melted butter, dredge with confectioners' sugar and cool on a wire rack.

teacakes

serves 12

prep: 30 mins, plus 3 hrs rising/cooling

cook: 20 mins

These popular tea snacks are ideal split in half and toasted, then spread with butter. Use a luxury mix of dry fruit, if possible.

INGREDIENTS

2 tbsp butter, cut into small pieces, plus
extra for greasing

3 cups strong white bread flour, plus
extra for dusting

¼-oz/7-g envelope active dry yeast

¼ cup superfine sugar

1 tsp salt

1¼ cups lukewarm milk

2¾ oz/75 g luxury dry fruit mix

honey, for brushing

butter, to serve

NUTRITIONAL INFORMATION

Calories	197
Protein	. . . . .6g
Carbohydrate	. . . . .39g
Sugars	. . . . .11g
Fat	. . . . .3g
Saturates	. . . . .2g

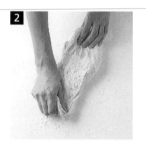

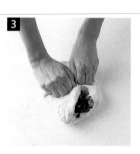

cook's tip

It is important to have the milk at the right temperature. Heat it until you can put your little finger into the milk and leave it there for 10 seconds without it feeling too hot.

1 Grease several cookie sheets with a little butter. Sift the flour into a large bowl. Stir in the yeast, sugar, and salt. Add the butter and rub it in with your fingertips until the mixture resembles fine bread crumbs. Add the milk and mix together to form a soft dough.

2 Place the dough on a lightly floured counter and knead for 5 minutes. Alternatively, knead the dough with an electric mixer with a dough hook. Place the dough in a greased bowl, cover, and let rise in a warm place for 1–1½ hours, or until it has doubled in size.

3 Knead the dough again for a few minutes, then knead in the fruit. Divide the dough into 12 circles and place on the cookie sheets. Cover and let stand for an additional 1 hour, or until springy to the touch.

4 Preheat the oven to 400°F/200°C, then bake the teacakes for 20 minutes. Brush with honey while still warm, then transfer the teacakes to a wire rack to cool completely before serving them split in half and toasted, if wished. Spread with butter and serve.

cinnamon swirls

cook: 30 mins

prep: 25 mins, plus 1 hr 20 mins rising/cooling

serves 12

These cinnamon-flavored buns are delicious if they are served warm a few minutes after they come out of the oven.

NUTRITIONAL INFORMATION

Calories 160

Protein 4g

Carbohydrate 24g

Sugars 10g

Fat 6g

Saturates 4g

INGREDIENTS

2 tbsp butter, cut into small pieces, plus extra for greasing

1½ cups strong white bread flour

½ tsp salt

¼-oz/7-g envelope active dry yeast

1 egg, beaten

½ cup warm milk

2 tbsp maple syrup

FILLING

4 tbsp butter, softened

2 tsp ground cinnamon

¼ cup firmly packed brown sugar

generous ¼ cup currants

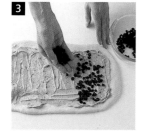

cook's tip

Instead of greasing the pan and bowl with butter, you can use a little vegetable or corn oil. Use a pastry brush to make sure that the pan and bowl are thoroughly oiled.

1 Grease a 9-inch/23-cm square cake pan. Sift the flour and salt into a bowl. Stir in the yeast. Rub in the butter with your fingertips until the mixture resembles fine bread crumbs. Add the egg and milk and mix to form a dough. Place in a greased bowl, cover, and let stand in a warm place for 40 minutes, or until doubled in size.

2 Knead the dough lightly for 1 minute to punch it down, then roll out on a lightly floured counter to a rectangle measuring 12 x 9 inches/30 x 23 cm.

3 To make the filling, beat the butter, cinnamon, and brown sugar together until the mixture is light and fluffy. Spread the filling over the dough, leaving a 1-inch/2.5-cm border all round. Sprinkle over the currants.

4 Carefully roll up the dough like a jelly roll, starting at a long edge, and press down to seal. Using a sharp knife, cut the roll into 12 slices. Place them in the prepared pan, cover, and let stand for 30 minutes.

5 Preheat the oven to 375°F/190°C, then bake the swirls for 20–30 minutes, or until well risen. Brush the swirls with the syrup and let cool slightly before serving warm.

hot cross buns

makes 12 **prep: 35 mins, plus 2 hrs 45 mins rising** **cook: 16–21 mins**

There is nothing more tempting than the mouthwatering aroma of warm, spicy hot cross buns straight from the oven.

INGREDIENTS

scant 4 cups strong white bread flour, plus extra for dusting

½ tsp salt

2 tsp ground allspice

1 tsp ground nutmeg

1 tsp ground cinnamon

2 tsp active dry yeast

¼ cup golden superfine sugar

finely grated rind of 1 lemon

scant 1¼ cups currants

scant ½ cup chopped candied peel

5½ tbsp butter, melted

1 egg

scant 1 cup tepid milk

vegetable oil, for brushing

CROSSES

6 tbsp all-purpose flour

2 tbsp butter, cut into pieces

1 tbsp cold water

GLAZE

3 tbsp milk

3 tbsp golden superfine sugar

NUTRITIONAL INFORMATION

Calories 323

Protein 7g

Carbohydrate 57g

Sugars 23g

Fat 9g

Saturates 5g

variation

If you would rather make mini hot cross buns, divide the dough into 24 pieces instead of 12.

cook's tip

Make sure that you press the dough crosses gently but firmly onto the buns, so that they do not separate while they are baking.

1 Sift the flour, salt, and spices into a bowl and stir in the yeast, sugar, lemon rind, currants, and candied peel. Make a well in the center. In a separate bowl, mix the melted butter, egg, and milk. Pour into the dry ingredients and mix to make a soft dough, adding more milk if necessary. Brush a bowl with oil. Turn the dough out onto a floured counter and knead for 10 minutes, or until smooth and elastic. Place the dough in the oiled bowl, cover with plastic wrap, and let stand in a warm place for 1¾–2 hours, or until doubled in size.

2 Turn out onto a floured counter, knead for 1–2 minutes, then divide into 12 balls. Place on a greased cookie sheet, flatten slightly, then cover with oiled plastic wrap. Let stand in a warm place for 45 minutes, or until doubled in size. Preheat the oven to 425°F/220°C.

3 To make the crosses, sift the flour into a bowl and rub in the butter. Stir in the cold water to make a dough. Divide into 24 strips, 7-inches/18-cm long. To make the glaze, place the milk and sugar in a pan over low heat and stir until the sugar has dissolved. Brush some of the glaze over the buns and lay the dough strips on them to form crosses. Bake in the oven for 15–20 minutes, or until golden. Brush with the remaining glaze and return to the oven for 1 minute. Cool on a wire rack.

caraway kugelhopf

serves 8

prep: 15 mins,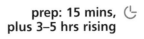
plus 3–5 hrs rising

cook: 30 mins

Kugelhopf is a traditional German specialty that is a cross between a bread and a cake. The addition of caraway seeds to the recipe gives this kugelhopf an unusual flavor.

INGREDIENTS

generous 1½ cups strong white bread flour

¼ cup golden superfine sugar

2 tsp active dry yeast

4 tsp caraway seeds

scant ¼ cup tepid water

4 oz/115 g butter, melted, plus extra for greasing

3 eggs, beaten

confectioners' sugar, for dusting

butter, to serve

NUTRITIONAL INFORMATION

Calories	.267
Protein	.7g
Carbohydrate	.29g
Sugars	.8g
Fat	.15g
Saturates	.9g

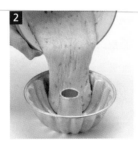

cook's tip

Because a kugelhopf mold has a lot of detailed indentations, it is important to grease it thoroughly so that it turns out easily. If you do not have a kugelhopf mold, use an ordinary ring mold.

1 Sift the flour into a warmed bowl and stir in the sugar, yeast, and caraway seeds. Make a well in the center. In a separate bowl, mix the water, butter, and eggs. Pour into the dry ingredients. Beat until smooth. Cover the bowl with plastic wrap and let stand in a warm place for 2–3 hours, or until the mixture has doubled in size.

2 Grease an 8-inch/20-cm kugelhopf mold. Stir the mixture and turn into the mold. Cover with plastic wrap and let rise again for 1–2 hours, or until doubled in size. Preheat the oven to 400°F/200°C.

3 Remove the plastic wrap and bake the kugelhopf in the preheated oven for 20 minutes. Reduce the oven temperature to 375°F/190°C and bake for an additional 10 minutes, or until well risen and golden brown. Let cool in the mold for 10 minutes, then turn out onto a wire rack to cool until warm. Dust with sifted confectioners' sugar and serve immediately with butter.

orange & raisin brioches

cook: 15 mins **prep: 30 mins, plus 2 hrs rising** **makes 12**

*Brioche is a light, rich French bread, which can be made as a loaf
or buns. It is usually served with coffee for breakfast, but with the
addition of raisins, it goes well served with butter and a cup of tea.*

NUTRITIONAL INFORMATION

Calories 129

Protein 4g

Carbohydrate 19g

Sugars 5g

Fat 5g

Saturates 3g

INGREDIENTS

2 oz/55 g butter, melted, plus

extra for greasing

generous 1½ cups strong white bread

flour, plus extra for dusting

½ tsp salt

2 tsp active dry yeast

1 tbsp golden superfine sugar

⅓ cup raisins

grated rind of 1 orange

2 tbsp tepid water

2 eggs, beaten

vegetable oil, for brushing

1 beaten egg, for glazing

cook's tip

If you do not have brioche
molds, you can use ordinary
bun pans instead—the buns
will not have patterned bases,
but they will taste just as good.

1 Grease 12 individual brioche molds. Sift the flour and salt into a warmed bowl and stir in the yeast, sugar, raisins, and orange rind. Make a well in the center. In a separate bowl, mix together the water, eggs, and melted butter and pour into the dry ingredients. Beat vigorously to make a soft dough. Turn out onto a lightly floured counter and knead for 5 minutes, or until smooth and elastic. Brush a clean bowl with oil. Place the dough in the bowl, cover with plastic wrap, and let stand in a warm place for 1 hour, or until doubled in size.

2 Turn out onto a floured counter, knead lightly for 1 minute, then roll into a rope shape. Cut into 12 equal pieces. Shape three-fourths of each piece into a ball and place in the prepared molds. With a floured finger, press a hole in the center of each. Shape the remaining pieces of dough into little plugs and press into the holes, flattening the top slightly.

3 Place the molds on a cookie sheet, cover lightly with oiled plastic wrap, and let stand in a warm place for 1 hour, until the dough comes almost to the top.

4 Preheat the oven to 425°F/220°C. Brush the brioches with beaten egg and bake in the preheated oven for 15 minutes, or until golden brown. Serve warm with butter, if you like.

chelsea buns

makes 9

prep: 30 mins, plus 1 hr 45 mins rising

cook: 30 mins

Sweet and sticky Chelsea buns, with a hint of spice, are an irresistible addition to a cup of afternoon tea.

INGREDIENTS

2 tbsp butter, plus extra for greasing

generous 1½ cups strong white bread flour, plus extra for dusting

½ tsp salt

2 tsp active dry yeast

1 tsp golden superfine sugar

½ cup tepid milk

1 egg, beaten

vegetable oil, for brushing

generous ¾ cup confectioners' sugar, to glaze

FILLING

¼ cup brown sugar

4 oz/115 g luxury mixed dry fruit

1 tsp ground allspice

2 oz/55 g butter, softened

NUTRITIONAL INFORMATION

Calories 266

Protein 5g

Carbohydrate 45g

Sugars 26g

Fat 9g

Saturates 5g

variation

For an extra spiciness, add ½ teaspoon ground cinnamon and ½ teaspoon freshly grated nutmeg to the filling.

cook's tip

When you place the buns in the prepared cake pan, place them close to each other in three rows, so that they join up into one single piece as they expand during cooking.

1 Grease a 7-inch/18-cm square cake pan. Sift the flour and salt into a warmed bowl, stir in the yeast and sugar, and rub in the butter. Make a well in the center. In a separate bowl, mix the milk and egg and pour into the dry ingredients. Beat to make a soft dough. Turn out onto a floured counter and knead for 5–10 minutes, or

until smooth. Brush a clean bowl with oil, place the dough in the bowl, cover with plastic wrap and let stand in a warm place for 1 hour, or until doubled in size.

2 Turn the dough out onto a floured counter and knead lightly for 1 minute. Roll out into a 12 x 9-inch/ 30 x 23-cm rectangle.

3 To make the filling, place the brown sugar, fruit, and spice in a bowl and mix. Spread the dough with the softened butter and sprinkle the fruit mixture on top. Roll up from a long side, then cut into 9 pieces. Place in the prepared pan, cut-side up. Cover with oiled plastic wrap and let stand in a warm place for 45 minutes, or until risen.

4 Preheat the oven to 375°F/190°C. Bake the buns in the oven for 30 minutes, or until golden. Let cool in the pan for 10 minutes, then transfer, in one piece, to a wire rack to cool. Sift the confectioners' sugar into a bowl and stir in enough water to make a thin glaze. Brush over the buns and let set. Pull the buns apart to serve.

apricot & walnut bread

serves 12

prep: 25 mins, ☽
plus 2–5 hrs rising

cook: 30 mins ⏻

*Serve this fruit bread freshly made, sliced and buttered,
or leave it whole and invite guests to break off tasty
morsels with their hands.*

INGREDIENTS

2 oz/55 g butter, plus extra
for greasing

generous 2½ cups strong white bread
flour, plus extra for dusting

½ tsp salt

1 tsp golden superfine sugar

2 tsp active dry yeast

generous ⅔ cup no-soak dried
apricots, chopped

⅓ cup chopped walnuts

⅔ cup tepid milk

scant ⅓ cup tepid water

1 egg, beaten

vegetable oil, for brushing

TOPPING

generous ¾ cup confectioners' sugar

walnut halves

variation

As an alternative to apricots, you
can substitute candied cherries, dried
cranberries, or dates.

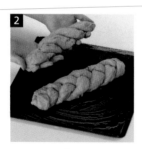

cook's tip

Braiding the bread in this way
makes it much easier to pull
the loaf apart into bite-size
pieces after cooking. Let the
loaf cool before eating.

1 Grease and flour a cookie sheet. Sift the flour and salt into a warmed bowl and stir in the sugar and yeast. Rub in the butter and add the chopped apricots and walnuts. Make a well in the center. In a separate bowl, mix together the milk, water, and egg. Pour into the dry ingredients and mix to a soft dough. Turn out onto a floured counter and knead for 10 minutes, or until smooth. Brush a clean bowl with oil, place the dough in the bowl, cover with oiled plastic wrap, and let stand in a warm place for 2–3 hours, or until doubled in size.

2 Turn the dough out onto a floured counter and knead lightly for 1 minute.

Divide into 5 equal pieces and roll each piece into a rope 12-inches/30-cm long. Braid 3 ropes together, pinching the ends to seal, and place on the prepared cookie sheet. Twist the remaining 2 ropes together and place on top. Cover lightly with oiled plastic wrap and let stand in a warm place for 1–2 hours, or until it has doubled in size.

3 Preheat the oven to 425°F/220°C. Bake the bread for 10 minutes, reduce the heat to 375°F/190°C, and bake for an additional 20 minutes. Transfer to a wire rack to cool. To make the topping, sift the confectioners' sugar into a bowl, stir in enough water to make a thin frosting and drizzle over the loaf. Decorate with walnuts.

barm brack

cook: 1 hr

prep: 25 mins, plus 2 hrs 30 mins rising

serves 15

variation

Change your choice of dry fruit for different flavors, using currants and raisins on their own, or mixed with chopped dried apricots or even figs.

This Irish spiced bread was once traditionally baked with a wedding ring thrown into the mixture in the belief that whoever received the ring would be married within the year.

INGREDIENTS

scant 5 cups strong white bread flour, plus extra for dusting

1 tsp ground allspice

1 tsp salt

2 tsp active dry yeast

¼ cup golden superfine sugar

1¼ cups tepid milk

⅔ cup tepid water

vegetable oil, for brushing

2 oz/55 g butter, softened, plus extra for greasing

11½ oz/325 g mixed dry fruit

milk, for glazing

cook's tip

Allowing the bread to rise three times gives it its particular open texture, but if time is short, you can omit the second rising.

1 Sift the flour, allspice, and salt into a warmed bowl, then stir in the yeast and 1 tablespoon of the superfine sugar. Make a well in the center and pour in the milk and water. Mix well, gradually incorporating the dry ingredients to make a sticky dough. Place on a lightly floured counter and knead

until no longer sticky. Brush a clean, warmed bowl with oil, place the dough in the bowl, cover with plastic wrap and let stand in a warm place for 1 hour, or until doubled in size.

2 Turn the dough out onto a work counter and knead lightly for 1 minute. Add the butter and mixed fruit

to the dough and work them in well. Return the dough to the bowl, replace the plastic wrap, and let rise for 30 minutes. Grease a 9-inch/23-cm round cake pan. Shape the dough into a circle and fit in the pan. Cover and let stand in a warm place until it has risen to the top of the pan. Preheat the oven to 400°F/200°C.

3 Brush the top of the loaf lightly with milk and bake in the preheated oven for 15 minutes. Cover the loaf with foil, reduce the oven temperature to 350°F/180°C, and bake for 45 minutes, or until the bread is golden and sounds hollow when tapped on the bottom. Transfer to a wire rack to cool.

marbled chocolate & orange teabread

serves 12

prep: 20 mins, plus 20 mins cooling

cook: 35–40 mins

This recipe makes two cakes: one to eat straight away and one to freeze and keep for another day.

INGREDIENTS

5 oz/140 g butter, softened, plus extra for greasing

2¾ oz/75 g semisweet chocolate, broken into pieces

1¼ cups golden superfine sugar

5 large eggs, beaten

generous 1 cup all-purpose flour

2 tsp baking powder

pinch of salt

grated rind of 2 oranges

NUTRITIONAL INFORMATION

Calories	286
Protein	..............5g
Carbohydrate	.........36g
Sugars	..............26g
Fat	.................15g
Saturates	..............9g

1 Preheat the oven to 350°F/180°C. Grease and line the bottom and ends of 2 x 1-lb/450-g loaf pans. Place the chocolate in a bowl set over a pan of simmering water, making sure that the bottom of the bowl does not touch the water. Remove from the heat once the chocolate has melted.

2 Place the butter and sugar in a separate bowl and beat until light and fluffy. Gradually beat in the eggs. Sift the flour, baking powder, and salt into the mixture and fold in.

3 Transfer one-third of the mixture to the melted chocolate and stir.

Stir the orange rind into the remaining mixture and spread one-fourth of the mixture evenly in each cake pan.

4 Drop spoonfuls of the chocolate mixture on top, dividing it between the 2 pans, but do not smooth it out. Divide the remaining orange mixture between the

2 pans, then, using a knife, gently swirl the top 2 layers together to give a marbled effect. Bake in the preheated oven for 35–40 minutes, or until a skewer inserted into the center comes out clean. Let cool in the pans for 10 minutes, then turn out, peel off the lining paper, and transfer to a wire rack to cool completely.

cook's tip

When you add the beaten eggs gradually in Step 2, the mixture may appear to curdle. Don't worry, this is perfectly normal.

date & walnut teabread

**cook: 1 hr 5 mins–
1 hr 20 mins**

**prep: 20 mins, plus
20 mins cooling**

serves 10

*This moist and delightful teabread has sticky layers of sweet
date purée running through it.*

NUTRITIONAL INFORMATION

Calories 396

Protein 6g

Carbohydrate 46g

Sugars 35g

Fat 22g

Saturates 11g

INGREDIENTS

6 oz/175 g butter, plus extra
for greasing

scant 1⅓ cups pitted dates, chopped
into small pieces

grated rind and juice of 1 orange

scant ¼ cup water

scant 1 cup brown sugar

3 eggs, beaten

⅔ cup whole-wheat self-rising flour

⅔ cup white self-rising flour

⅓ cup chopped walnuts

8 walnut halves

orange zest, to decorate

cook's tip

Dates sold specifically for
baking are often rolled in
sugar; do not use these, as
they will make the teabread
taste too sweet.

1 Preheat the oven
to 325°F/160°C. Grease
and line the bottom and ends
of a 2-lb/900-g loaf pan. Place
the dates in a pan with the
orange rind and juice and
water and cook over medium
heat for 5 minutes, stirring, or
until it is a soft purée.

2 Place the butter and
sugar in a bowl and
beat together until light and
fluffy. Gradually beat in the
eggs, then sift in the flours
and fold in with the chopped
walnuts. Spread one-third of
the mixture over the bottom
of the prepared loaf pan and
spread half the date purée
over the top.

3 Repeat the layers,
ending with the cake
mixture. Arrange walnut
halves on top. Bake in the oven
for 1–1¼ hours, or until well
risen and firm to the touch. Let
cool in the pan for 10 minutes.
Turn out, peel off the lining
paper, and transfer to a wire
rack to cool. Decorate with
orange zest and serve in slices.

cinnamon & currant loaf

serves 8   **prep: 25 mins, plus 1 hr cooling**   **cook: 1 hr 10 mins**

This spicy, fruit teabread is quick and easy to make. Serve it buttered and with a drizzle of honey for an afternoon snack.

INGREDIENTS

5½ oz/150 g butter, cut into small pieces, plus extra for greasing

2¼ cups all-purpose flour

pinch of salt

1 tbsp baking powder

1 tbsp ground cinnamon

generous ⅜ cup brown sugar

1 cup currants

finely grated rind of 1 orange

5–6 tbsp orange juice

6 tbsp milk

2 eggs, lightly beaten

NUTRITIONAL INFORMATION	
Calories	.439
Protein	.7g
Carbohydrate	.67g
Sugars	.33g
Fat	.18g
Saturates	.11g

variation

You can replace the currants with raisins or golden raisins or a mixture of both, if you prefer.

cook's tip

Once you have added the liquid to the dry ingredients, work as quickly as possible because the baking powder is activated by the liquid.

1 Preheat the oven to 350°F/180°C. Grease a 2-lb/900-g loaf pan and line the bottom with parchment paper.

2 Sift the flour, salt, baking powder, and cinnamon into a bowl. Rub in the butter with your fingers until the mixture resembles coarse bread crumbs.

3 Stir in the sugar, currants, and orange rind. Beat the orange juice, milk and eggs together and add to the dry ingredients. Mix well. Spoon into the pan and make a slight dip in the center to help it rise evenly.

4 Bake in the preheated oven for 1–1 hour 10 minutes, or until a fine metal skewer inserted into the center of the loaf comes out clean. Let the loaf cool in the pan for 10 minutes, then turn out onto a wire rack to cool completely before slicing and serving.

spiced apple & apricot tea loaf

serves 10 **prep: 15 mins, plus 10 mins cooling** **cook: 55–60 mins**

The firm texture of this cake makes it an ideal fruity snack for picnic hampers and children's lunch boxes.

INGREDIENTS

4 oz/115 g butter, softened, plus extra for greasing

scant ¾ cup brown sugar

2 eggs, beaten

scant ⅓ cup no-soak dried apricots, chopped

2 eating apples, peeled and coarsely grated

2 tbsp milk

generous 1½ cups self-rising flour

1 tsp ground allspice

½ tsp ground cinnamon

NUTRITIONAL INFORMATION

Calories 258

Protein 4g

Carbohydrate 38g

Sugars 21g

Fat 11g

Saturates 7g

cook's tip

No-soak dried apricots are sold in most large food stores as "ready-to-eat" dried apricots, and are soft enough to chop very easily.

1 Preheat the oven to 350°F/180°C. Grease and line the bottom and ends of a 2-lb/900-g loaf pan. Place the butter and sugar in a bowl and beat until light and fluffy. Gradually beat in the eggs.

2 Reserve 1 tablespoon of the apricots, then fold the rest into the creamed mixture with the grated apples and milk. Sift in the flour, allspice, and cinnamon and fold into the mixture.

3 Spoon into the prepared pan and sprinkle over the reserved apricots. Bake in the preheated oven for 55–60 minutes, or until risen and a skewer inserted into the center comes out clean. Let cool in the pan for 10 minutes, then turn out and peel off the lining paper. Transfer to a wire rack to cool completely.

sticky ginger marmalade loaf

cook: 1 hr

prep: 10 mins, plus 10 mins cooling

serves 10

Ginger marmalade gives a wonderful warming flavor to this moist, sticky teabread, perfect with a cup of afternoon tea.

NUTRITIONAL INFORMATION

Calories 399

Protein 5g

Carbohydrate 45g

Sugars 28g

Fat 23g

Saturates 11g

INGREDIENTS

6 oz/175 g butter, softened, plus extra for greasing

⅓ cup ginger marmalade

scant 1 cup brown sugar

3 eggs, beaten

generous 1½ cups self-rising flour

½ tsp baking powder

1 tsp ground ginger

⅔ cup coarsely chopped pecans

cook's tip

If the marmalade loaf starts to brown too much before it has finished cooking, cover the top lightly with a piece of foil.

1 Preheat the oven to 350°F/180°C. Grease and line the bottom and ends of a 2-lb/900-g loaf pan. Place 1 tablespoon of the ginger marmalade in a small pan and reserve. Place the remaining marmalade in a bowl with the butter, sugar, and eggs.

2 Sift in the flour, baking powder, and ground ginger and beat together until smooth. Stir in three-quarters of the nuts. Spoon the mixture into the prepared loaf pan and smooth the top. Sprinkle with the remaining nuts and bake in the preheated oven for 1 hour, or until well risen and a skewer inserted into the center comes out clean.

3 Let cool in the pan for 10 minutes, then turn out and peel off the lining paper. Transfer to a wire rack to cool until warm. Set the pan of reserved marmalade over low heat to warm, then brush over the loaf and serve in slices.

banana & chocolate chip loaf

serves 10

prep: 25 mins, plus 30 mins cooling

cook: 1 hr 10 mins

Bananas make this loaf cake beautifully moist, and combining them with chocolate makes this sweet bread a favorite with children.

INGREDIENTS

4 oz/115 g butter, softened, plus extra for greasing

1¼ cups all-purpose flour

1 tsp baking soda

pinch of salt

1 tsp ground cinnamon

scant 1 cup golden superfine sugar

2 large ripe bananas, mashed

2 eggs, beaten

5 tbsp boiling water

1 cup semisweet chocolate chips

TO SERVE

whipped cream

ready-made chocolate decorations

NUTRITIONAL INFORMATION

Calories 344

Protein 4g

Carbohydrate 49g

Sugars 34g

Fat 16g

Saturates 10g

variation

Substituting milk chocolate chips for the semisweet chips will give the loaf a slightly richer taste.

cook's tip

Because this is a very moist cake, it is not possible to test with a skewer, which will always come out sticky.

1 Preheat the oven to 325°F/160°C. Grease and line the bottom and sides of a 2-lb/900-g loaf pan. Sift the flour, baking soda, salt, and cinnamon into a bowl and set aside. Place the butter and sugar in a bowl and beat together until light and fluffy.

2 Beat in the bananas and then the eggs. The mixture may look curdled, but this is perfectly normal. Stir in the flour mixture alternately with the boiling water until just combined, then stir in the chocolate chips.

3 Spoon into the prepared pan and smooth the top. Bake in the preheated oven for 1 hour 10 minutes, or until well risen, golden brown, and firm to the touch. Let cool in the pan for 30 minutes, then turn out and peel off the lining paper. Transfer to a wire rack to cool completely, then serve in slices with a little whipped cream, decorated with chocolate decorations.

glossy fruit loaf

cook: 1 hr 30 mins– 1 hr 45 mins

prep: 20 mins, plus 8 hrs 20 mins soaking/cooling

serves 10

NUTRITIONAL INFORMATION

Calories 400

Protein 6g

Carbohydrate 53g

Sugars 39g

Fat 20g

Saturates 9g

variation

Try using several different types of dry fruit and nuts, according to your personal taste.

This is a rich, sweet fruit loaf, ideal for family celebrations or parties, and tastes superb with a cup of hot tea.

INGREDIENTS

⅓ cup raisins

½ cup no-soak dried apricots, coarsely chopped

⅓ cup pitted dates, chopped

⅓ cup cold black tea

4 oz/115 g butter, plus extra for greasing

generous ½ cup brown sugar

2 eggs, beaten

1¼ cups self-rising flour, sifted

scant ⅓ cup coarsely chopped candied pineapple

scant ½ cup candied cherries, halved

generous ½ cup coarsely chopped Brazil nuts

TOPPING

¼ cup walnut halves

scant ¼ cup Brazil nuts

¼ cup candied cherries, halved

2 tbsp apricot jelly, strained

cook's tip

Soaking dry fruit in cold black tea makes the fruit plump and juicy, which gives fruit-bread an extra flavor and moistness.

1 Place the raisins, apricots, and dates in a bowl, pour over the tea, cover, and let soak for 8 hours, or overnight. Preheat the oven to 325°F/160°C. Grease and line the bottom and ends of a 2-lb/900-g loaf pan. Place the butter and sugar in a bowl and beat together until light and fluffy.

2 Gradually beat in the eggs, then fold in the flour alternately with the soaked fruit. Gently stir in the pineapple, cherries, and chopped nuts. Turn the mixture into the prepared pan. To make the topping, arrange the walnuts, Brazil nuts, and cherries on top.

3 Bake in the preheated oven for 1½–1¾ hours, or until a skewer inserted into the center comes out clean. Let cool in the pan for 10 minutes, then turn out and peel off the lining paper. Transfer to a wire rack to cool completely. Warm the apricot jelly and brush over the top of the cake.

date & honey loaf

serves 10   **prep: 15 mins, plus 1 hr 50 mins rising/cooling**   **cook: 30 mins**

This bread is full of good things—chopped dates, sesame seeds, and honey. Toast thick slices and spread with soft cheese.

INGREDIENTS

butter, for greasing

1¾ cups strong white bread flour, plus extra for dusting

½ cup strong brown bread flour

½ tsp salt

¼-oz/7-g envelope active dry yeast

scant 1 cup lukewarm water

3 tbsp corn oil

3 tbsp honey

½ cup dried dates, chopped

2 tbsp sesame seeds

NUTRITIONAL INFORMATION	
Calories	240
Protein	6g
Carbohydrate	44g
Sugars	14g
Fat	6g
Saturates	1g

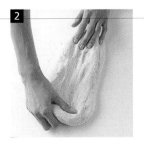

cook's tip

If you cannot find a warm place, sit a bowl with the dough in it over a pan of warm water and cover and leave until the dough has doubled in size.

1 Grease a 2-lb/900-g loaf pan with butter. Sift the white and brown flours into a large bowl and stir in the salt and yeast. Pour in the water, oil, and honey and mix to form a dough.

2 Place the dough on a lightly floured counter and knead for 5 minutes, or until smooth, then place in a greased bowl. Cover and let rise in a warm place for 1 hour, or until doubled in size.

3 Knead in the dates and sesame seeds. Shape the dough and place in the prepared pan. Cover and let stand in a warm place for an additional 30 minutes, or until springy to the touch.

4 Preheat the oven to 425°F/220°C, then bake the loaf for 30 minutes, or until a hollow sound is heard when the bottom of the loaf is tapped.

5 Transfer the loaf to a wire rack and let cool completely. Serve cut into thick slices.

pumpkin loaf

cook: 2 hrs **prep: 30 mins, plus 1 hr cooling** **serves 6**

The pumpkin purée in this loaf makes it beautifully moist. It is delicious eaten at any time of the day.

NUTRITIONAL INFORMATION

Calories 465

Protein 7g

Carbohydrate 62g

Sugars 33g

Fat 21g

Saturates 12g

INGREDIENTS

vegetable oil, for oiling

1 lb/450 g pumpkin flesh

4½ oz/125 g butter, softened, plus extra for greasing

generous ¾ cup superfine sugar

2 eggs, beaten

1½ cups all-purpose flour, sifted

1½ tsp baking powder

½ tsp salt

1 tsp ground allspice

⅛ cup pepitas

cook's tip

To ensure that the pumpkin purée is dry, place it in a pan over medium heat for a few minutes, stirring frequently, until it is thick.

1 Preheat the oven to 400°F/200°C. Brush a 2-lb/900-g loaf pan with vegetable oil.

2 Chop the pumpkin into large pieces and wrap in buttered foil. Bake in the oven for 30–40 minutes, or until tender. Let the pumpkin cool completely before mashing to a thick purée.

3 Beat the butter and sugar together in a large bowl until light and fluffy. Add the eggs a little at a time. Stir in the pumpkin purée. Fold in the flour, baking powder, salt, and allspice.

4 Fold the pepitas gently through the mixture. Spoon the mixture into the prepared loaf pan.

5 Reduce the oven temperature to 325°F/160°C, then bake the loaf for 1¼–1½ hours, or until a skewer inserted into the center of the loaf comes out clean. Let the loaf cool before serving.

pies, tarts & pastries

At the beginning of this book are recipes for basic pastries that are simple to make, especially if you use a food processor. However, if you are nervous about making pastry, there is no need to avoid baking the recipes in this section, as it is easy to buy excellent ready-made pastries. When it comes to puff pastry or phyllo pastry, most people will be happy to use the ready-prepared varieties.

In this section, you will find recipes from all over the world, such as a fresh and light Sicilian Ricotta Tart (see page 129), family favorite Pecan Pie (see page 108), and a gloriously sticky Baklava (see page 118) from Greece. Some of the easiest recipes are those made with phyllo pastry, such as Pear & Pecan Strudel (see page 128), where the pastry is simply rolled round a filling, without the need for rolling out or lining tart pans. There are recipes for every occasion, such as an Orange Syrup Tart (see page 117) or Coconut Tart (see page 106) for a family lunch, and fashionable Tarte au Citron (see page 114) or a rich Chocolate, Chestnut & Ginger Tart (see page 130) for a dinner party. Individual tarts and pastries look very attractive served as a dessert and are also perfect for serving with a cup of coffee or tea. Summer Fruit Tartlets (see page 126) or Raspberry Eclairs (see page 122) would be an ideal al fresco treat when the sun is shining. There are also recipes for savory pastries. Crab & Ginger Triangles (see page 134) are a delicious accompaniment to drinks, Phyllo Tarts with Avocado Salsa (see page 135) and Mini Choux Puffs with Shrimp Cocktail (see page 136) are ideal appetizers, and Greek Feta & Olive Tarts (see page 138) make a quick and easy lunch served with salad.

banana pastries

cook: 25 mins

prep: 20 mins, plus 30 mins chilling

serves 4

These pastries require a little time to prepare, but are well worth the effort. A sweet banana filling is wrapped in dough and baked.

INGREDIENTS

PIE DOUGH

3 cups all-purpose flour

4 tbsp shortening

4 tbsp unsalted butter

½ cup water

FILLING

2 large bananas

½ cup finely chopped no-soak dried apricots

pinch of nutmeg

dash of orange juice

1 egg yolk, beaten

confectioners' sugar, for dusting

cream or ice cream, to serve

variation

Use a fruit filling of your choice, such as apple or plum as an alternative. Replace the nutmeg with ground cinnamon, if you prefer.

cook's tip

Brush the pastries with 1–2 tablespoons of milk instead of the beaten egg, if you prefer. The cooked pastries will turn a pale golden color.

1 To make the pie dough, sift the flour into a large bowl. Add the shortening and butter and rub into the flour with your fingertips until the mixture resembles bread crumbs. Gradually blend in the water to form a soft dough. Wrap in plastic wrap and let chill in the refrigerator for 30 minutes.

2 Preheat the oven to 350°F/180°C. Mash the bananas in a bowl with a fork and stir in the apricots, nutmeg, and orange juice, mixing well.

3 Roll the dough out on a lightly floured counter and cut out 16 circles 4-inches/10-cm in diameter.

4 Spoon a little of the banana filling onto one half of each circle and fold the dough over the filling to make semicircles. Pinch the edges together and seal by pressing with the prongs of a fork. Arrange the pastries on a nonstick cookie sheet and brush them with the beaten egg yolk. Cut a small slit in each pastry and bake in the preheated oven for 25 minutes, or until golden brown and crisp. Dust the banana pastries with confectioners' sugar and serve hot with cream or ice cream.

crème brûlée tarts

serves 6   **prep: 20 mins, plus**   **cook: 25 mins**
                     9 hrs chilling

An unusual dessert, serve these melt-in-the-mouth tarts with fresh mixed summer berries and a spoonful of ice cream or whipped cream, if you like.

INGREDIENTS

PIE DOUGH

1 cup all-purpose flour, plus extra for dusting

1–2 tbsp superfine sugar

4½ oz/125 g butter, cut into pieces

1 tbsp water

FILLING

4 egg yolks

¼ cup superfine sugar

1¾ cups heavy cream

1 tsp vanilla extract

raw brown sugar, for sprinkling

NUTRITIONAL INFORMATION

Calories	635
Protein	. . . . .6g
Carbohydrate	. . . . .36g
Sugars	. . . . .17g
Fat	. . . . .53g
Saturates	. . . . .32g

cook's tip

For best results, use cold butter, cut into small, even-size pieces. Make sure the butter is removed from the refrigerator before using because this will make it easier to handle.

1 To make the pie dough, place the flour and sugar in a large bowl. Rub in the butter with your fingertips until the mixture resembles bread crumbs. Add the water and mix to form a soft dough. Wrap and chill for 30 minutes.

2 Divide the dough into 6 pieces. Roll out each piece on a lightly floured counter to line 6 tart pans 4-inches/10-cm wide. Prick the bottom of the pastry with a fork and chill for 20 minutes.

3 Preheat the oven to 375°F/190°C. Line the pastry shells with foil and baking beans or pie weights and bake in the oven for 15 minutes. Remove the foil and baking beans and cook the pastry shells for an additional 10 minutes, or until crisp. Let cool. To make the filling, beat the egg yolks and sugar together in a bowl until pale. Heat the cream and vanilla extract in a pan until just below boiling point, then pour it onto the egg mixture, whisking constantly. Return the mixture to a clean pan and bring to just below a boil, stirring, until thick. Do not allow the mixture to boil or it will curdle. Let cool slightly, then pour it into the tart pans. Let cool, then chill overnight.

4 Preheat the broiler. Sprinkle the tarts with the sugar. Cook under the hot broiler for a few minutes. Let cool, then let chill for 2 hours before serving.

paper-thin fruit pies

cook: 15 mins   **prep: 20 mins**   **serves 4**

Perfect for weight watchers, these crisp pastry shells, filled with fruit and glazed with apricot jelly, are best served hot with lowfat custard.

NUTRITIONAL INFORMATION	
Calories	158
Protein	2g
Carbohydrate	14g
Sugars	12g
Fat	10g
Saturates	2g

INGREDIENTS

1 eating apple

1 ripe pear

2 tbsp lemon juice

2 oz/55 g lowfat spread

8 oz/225 g phyllo pastry, thawed if frozen

2 tbsp low-sugar apricot jelly

1 tbsp unsweetened orange juice

1 tbsp finely chopped pistachios

2 tsp confectioners' sugar, for dusting

lowfat custard, to serve

variation

Other combinations of fruit are equally delicious. Try peach and apricot, raspberry and apple, or pineapple and mango.

1 Preheat the oven to 400°F/200°C. Core and thinly slice the apple and pear and toss them in the lemon juice.

2 Melt the lowfat spread in a small pan over low heat. Cut the sheets of pastry into 4 and cover with a clean, damp dish towel. Brush 4 nonstick shallow pans, measuring 4 inch/10 cm across, with a little of the lowfat spread.

3 Working on each pie separately, brush 4 sheets of pastry with lowfat spread. Press a small sheet of pastry into the bottom of one pan. Arrange the other sheets of pastry on top at slightly different angles. Repeat with the remaining sheets of pastry to make another 3 pies. Arrange the apple and pear slices alternately in the center of each pastry shell and lightly crimp the edges of the pastry of each pie.

4 Mix the jelly and orange juice together until smooth and brush over the fruit. Bake in the preheated oven for 12–15 minutes. Sprinkle with the pistachios, dust lightly with confectioners' sugar and serve hot with lowfat custard.

coconut tart

serves 8   **prep: 25 mins,** ⏱ **plus 1 hr cooling**   **cook: 55 mins** 🔥

Coconut makes the filling in this tart lovely and moist. Serve it as a refreshing end to a heavy main meal.

INGREDIENTS

butter, for greasing

all-purpose flour, for dusting

1 quantity Sweet Pie Dough

(see page 13)

FILLING

2 eggs

grated rind and juice of 2 lemons

1 cup golden superfine sugar

1⅓ cups heavy cream

2¾ cups dry unsweetened coconut

NUTRITIONAL INFORMATION

Calories 772

Protein 7g

Carbohydrate 59g

Sugars 38g

Fat 58g

Saturates 40g

---

variation

Add ½ teaspoon of nutmeg to the filling mixture to give the tart a little extra flavor, if you like.

cook's tip

This coconut tart tastes exceptionally good if you serve it accompanied by a fresh passion fruit purée. Dry unsweetened coconut is usually available in large food stores.

1 Preheat the oven to 400°F/200°C, then grease a 9-inch/23-cm tart pan. On a lightly floured counter, roll out the pastry and use it to line the prepared pan, then bake blind (see page 13). Reduce the oven temperature to 325°F/160°C and place a cookie sheet in the oven.

2 To make the filling, place the eggs, lemon rind, and sugar in a bowl and beat together for 1 minute. Gently stir in the cream, then the lemon juice, and finally the coconut.

3 Spoon the filling into the tart shell and place the tart pan on the preheated cookie sheet. Bake in the oven for 40 minutes, or until set and golden. Let cool for 1 hour to firm up. Serve at room temperature.

pecan pie

serves 8　　　　**prep: 25 mins**　　　　**cook: 50 mins–**
1 hr 5 mins

Pecan pie is a variation on the traditional British treacle tart, and makes a rich and satisfying dessert.

INGREDIENTS

butter, for greasing

all-purpose flour, for dusting

1 quantity Sweet Pie Dough

(see page 13)

FILLING

3 eggs

generous 1 cup brown sugar

1 tsp vanilla extract

pinch of salt

6 tbsp butter, melted

3 tbsp corn syrup

3 tbsp molasses

1½ cups coarsely chopped pecans

pecan halves, to decorate

cream or vanilla ice cream, to serve

NUTRITIONAL INFORMATION

Calories 730

Protein 9g

Carbohydrate 74g

Sugars 53g

Fat 46g

Saturates 17g

variation

For a party-style pecan pie, pipe whipped cream over the surface in a decorative pattern before serving.

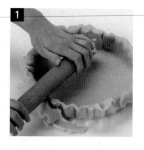

cook's tip

If the tart shell is becoming too brown while the pie is cooking, cover the pie with aluminum foil to prevent it burning.

1 Preheat the oven to 400°F/200°C, then grease a 9–10-inch/23–25-cm tart pan. On a lightly floured counter, roll out the pastry and use it to line the prepared pan, then bake blind (see page 13). Reduce the oven temperature to 350°F/180°C and place a cookie sheet in the oven.

2 To make the filling, place the eggs in a bowl and beat lightly. Beat in the sugar, vanilla extract, and salt. Stir in the melted butter, syrup, molasses, and chopped nuts. Pour into the tart shell and decorate with nut halves.

3 Place the tart pan on the preheated cookie sheet and bake in the oven for 35–40 minutes, or until the filling is set. Serve warm or at room temperature with cream or vanilla ice cream.

custard tart

serves 8   **prep: 15 mins, plus 1 hr chilling**   **cook: 1 hr**

This is a classic egg custard tart, which should be served as fresh as possible for the best flavor and texture.

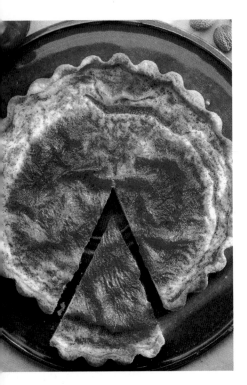

INGREDIENTS

PIE DOUGH

1 cup all-purpose flour, plus extra for dusting

1–2 tbsp superfine sugar

4½ oz/125 g butter, cut into pieces

1 tbsp water

FILLING

3 eggs

⅔ cup light cream

⅔ cup milk

freshly grated nutmeg

whipping cream, to serve

NUTRITIONAL INFORMATION

Calories	.268
Protein	.5g
Carbohydrate	.20g
Sugars	.5g
Fat	.19g
Saturates	.12g

cook's tip

Baking the pastry shell blind ensures that the finished tart has a crisp bottom. If you don't have foil, then use waxed paper instead.

1 To make the pie dough, place the flour and sugar in a large bowl and rub in the butter with your fingertips until the mixture resembles bread crumbs.

2 Add the water and mix together to form a soft dough. Wrap in plastic wrap and let chill in the refrigerator for 30 minutes.

3 Roll out the dough on a lightly floured counter to form a circle slightly larger than a 9½-inch/24-cm loose-bottom tart pan, then use to line the pan. Prick the dough with a fork and let chill for 30 minutes.

4 Preheat the oven to 375°F/190°C. Line the pastry shell with foil and baking beans or pie weights and bake in the oven for 15 minutes. Remove the foil and baking beans and bake the pastry shell for an additional 15 minutes.

5 To make the filling, whisk the eggs, cream, milk, and nutmeg together. Pour the filling into the prepared pastry shell. Return the tart to the oven and cook for 25–30 minutes, or until just set. Serve with whipping cream, if wished.

pear tarts

cook: 20 mins

prep: 10 mins, plus 30 mins chilling

serves 6

These tarts are made with ready-made puff pastry which is available from most supermarkets. The finished pastry is rich and buttery.

NUTRITIONAL INFORMATION

Calories	.250
Protein	.3g
Carbohydrate	.30g
Sugars	.15g
Fat	.14g
Saturates	.3g

INGREDIENTS

9 oz/250 g ready-made puff pastry, thawed if frozen

all-purpose flour, for dusting

1–2 tbsp brown sugar

2 tbsp butter, plus extra for brushing

1 tbsp finely chopped preserved ginger

3 pears, peeled, halved, and cored

cream, to serve

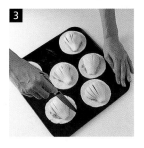

variation

If you prefer, serve these tarts with vanilla ice cream or a spoonful of whipped cream or sour cream for a delicious dessert.

1 Roll out the pastry on a lightly floured counter. Cut out 6 x 4-inch/ 10-cm circles with a plain cutter, then place the circles on a large cookie sheet and let chill in the refrigerator for 30 minutes.

2 Preheat the oven to 400°F/200°C. Beat the brown sugar and butter together in a small bowl, then stir in the chopped preserved ginger. Prick the pastry circles with a fork and spread a little of the ginger mixture onto each one.

3 Slice the pear halves lengthwise, keeping the pears intact at the tip. Fan out the slices slightly. Place a fanned-out pear half on top of each pastry circle. Make small flutes round the edge of the pastry circles and brush each pear half with a little melted butter.

4 Bake in the oven for 15–20 minutes, or until the pastry is well risen and golden. Let cool slightly, then serve warm with cream.

plum & almond tart

cook: 50 mins–1 hr 5 mins   **prep: 30 mins**   **serves 8**

variation

As an alternative to plums, try substituting apricots, cherries, or halved and sliced pears.

The flavors of plums and almonds make a particularly good combination in this delicious, warm tart.

INGREDIENTS

butter, for greasing

all-purpose flour, for dusting

1 quantity Sweet Pie Dough (see page 13)

FILLING

1 egg

1 egg yolk

scant ¾ cup golden superfine sugar

2 oz/55 g butter, melted

generous 1 cup ground almonds

1 tbsp brandy

2 lb/900 g plums, halved and pitted

whipped cream, to serve (optional)

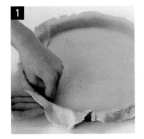  

cook's tip

The plum halves need to fit together tightly because they shrink during the baking process, so make sure that there are no large gaps.

1 Preheat the oven to 400°F/200°C, then grease a 9-inch/23-cm tart pan. On a lightly floured counter, roll out the pastry and use it to line the tart pan, then bake blind (see page 13). Place a cookie sheet in the oven.

2 To make the filling, place the egg, egg yolk, ½ cup of the superfine sugar, melted butter, ground almonds, and brandy in a bowl and mix together to form a paste. Spread the paste in the tart shell.

3 Arrange the plum halves, cut-side up, on top of the almond paste, fitting them together tightly. Sprinkle with the remaining superfine sugar. Place the tart pan on the preheated cookie sheet and bake in the oven for 35–40 minutes, or until the filling is set and the tart shell is brown. Serve warm with whipped cream, if you like.

tarte au citron

serves 6

prep: 20 mins, plus 15 mins cooling

cook: 40–55 mins

This smooth, creamy tart with the tangy fresh flavor of lemons makes the perfect end to a dinner party.

INGREDIENTS

butter, for greasing

all-purpose flour, for dusting

1 quantity Pâté Sucrée (see page 13)

FILLING

1 large egg

4 large egg yolks

scant ¾ cup golden superfine sugar

finely grated rind and juice

of 4 lemons (the juice should

measure ⅔ cup)

⅔ cup heavy cream

confectioners' sugar, for dusting

NUTRITIONAL INFORMATION

Calories 580

Protein 8g

Carbohydrate 65g

Sugars 37g

Fat 34g

Saturates 20g

variation

Reserve some of the lemon rind and sprinkle it over the tart after cooking for extra decoration.

cook's tip

The surface of the tart should not color. If it threatens to do so while baking, cover the top loosely with a piece of foil.

1 Preheat the oven to 400°F/200°C, then grease a 9-inch/23-cm tart pan. On a lightly floured counter, roll out the pastry and use it to line the tart pan,then bake blind (see page 13). Reduce the oven temperature to 325°F/160°C and place a cookie sheet in the oven.

2 To make the filling, place the egg, egg yolks, and sugar in a bowl and whisk until smooth. Gently stir in the lemon rind, lemon juice, and cream. Pour most of the filling into the tart shell, then place the tart pan on the preheated cookie sheet in the oven and spoon in the rest of the filling.

3 Bake in the oven for 25–30 minutes, or until there is no sign of liquid movement in the filling. Let cool in the pan for 15 minutes and serve warm or chilled. Before serving, sift over the confectioners' sugar to dust.

pear & cardamom tarte tatin

serves 4   **prep: 20 mins**   **cook: 30–35 mins**

This is a variation on a classic French apple tart, said to have been invented by the Tatin sisters. One of them dropped an apple tart when putting it in the oven and had to cook it upside-down!

INGREDIENTS

2 oz/55 g butter, softened

¼ cup golden superfine sugar

seeds from 10 cardamom pods

all-purpose flour, for dusting

8 oz/225 g ready-made puff pastry, thawed if frozen

3 ripe pears

whipped cream, to serve

NUTRITIONAL INFORMATION

Calories	.414
Protein	.4g
Carbohydrate	.47g
Sugars	.26g
Fat	.25g
Saturates	.7g

cook's tip

It is best to choose fairly large, round pears for this fruit tart, rather than the more elongated varieties. Try to choose pears that are ripe and not too firm.

1 Preheat the oven to 425°F/220°C. Spread the butter over the bottom of a 7-inch/18-cm ovenproof omelet pan or heavy-bottom cake pan. Spread the sugar evenly over the butter and scatter the cardamom seeds over the sugar. On a floured counter, roll out the pastry into a circle slightly larger than the pan. Prick the pastry lightly,

place it on a plate, and chill while preparing the pears.

2 Peel the pears, cut in half lengthwise, and cut out the cores. Arrange the pears, rounded sides down, on the butter and sugar. Set the pan over medium heat until the sugar melts and starts to bubble with the butter and juice from the pears. If any

areas are browning more than others, move the pan, but do not stir. As soon as the sugar has caramelized, remove the pan carefully from the heat.

3 Place the pastry on top, tucking the edges down the sides of the pan. Transfer to the oven and bake for 25 minutes, or until the pastry is well risen and golden. Leave

the tart in the pan for 2–3 minutes, or until the juices have stopped bubbling.

4 Invert the pan over a plate and shake to release the tart. It may be necessary to slide a spatula underneath the pears to loosen them. Serve the tart warm, with whipped cream.

orange syrup tart

cook: 30 mins   **prep: 20 mins**   **serves 6**

This delicious tart is made from a mixture of syrup and bread crumbs, which give it a delicious texture, and will make it a firm family favorite.

NUTRITIONAL INFORMATION	
Calories	275
Protein	3g
Carbohydrate	50g
Sugars	27g
Fat	8g
Saturates	4g

INGREDIENTS

butter, for greasing

all-purpose flour, for dusting

1 quantity Unsweetened Pie Dough
(see page 13)

FILLING

about ½ cup corn syrup

finely grated rind of 1 orange

1 tbsp orange juice

about 6 tbsp fresh white bread crumbs

cook's tip

When the tart is removed from the oven, the filling should still be on the soft side if the tart is to be eaten cold, because it hardens as it cools.

1 Grease an 8-inch/20-cm tart pan. On a lightly floured counter, roll out the pastry and use it to line the tart pan. Reserve the pastry trimmings. Preheat the oven to 375°F/190°C. To make the filling, place the syrup, orange rind, and orange juice in a pan over low heat and stir until the mixture is runny.

2 Remove the pan from the heat and stir in the bread crumbs. Let stand for 10 minutes, or until the bread crumbs have absorbed the syrup. If the mixture looks stodgy, add a little more syrup; if it looks thin, add some more bread crumbs. It should have the consistency of thick honey. Spread the mixture in the tart shell.

3 Roll out the pastry trimmings and cut into narrow strips. Use to make latticework across the top of the tart. Bake in the preheated oven for 30 minutes, or until the filling is almost set and the tart shell is brown. Serve warm or cold.

baklava

makes 20 pieces

**prep: 30 mins, plus
30 mins cooling**

cook: 40–50 mins

*Baklava is a traditional Greek pastry. Sticky and sweet and packed
with nuts, it makes a delicious dessert or accompaniment to coffee.*

INGREDIENTS

generous ⅔ cup blanched almonds

generous 1 cup walnuts

½ cup shelled pistachios

¼ cup brown sugar

1 tsp ground cinnamon

½ tsp freshly grated nutmeg

2 oz/55 g butter, melted, plus
extra for greasing

12 sheets ready-made phyllo pastry,
about 12 x 7 inches/30 x 18 cm

SYRUP

generous 1 cup granulated sugar

⅔ cup water

1 tbsp lemon juice

1 tbsp orange-flower water

NUTRITIONAL INFORMATION

Calories	190
Protein	3g
Carbohydrate	20g
Sugars	15g
Fat	11g
Saturates	2g

variation

You can vary the combination of nuts
used for the filling. Try using Brazil
nuts or pecans instead.

cook's tip

When chopping the nuts in the
food processor, take care not
to chop them into a powder—
the baklava needs to have a
crunchy texture.

1 To make the syrup,
place the sugar,
water, and lemon juice in a
pan over low heat and stir
until the sugar has completely
dissolved, then boil gently
for 5 minutes, until the
mixture takes on a syrupy
consistency. Add the orange-
flower water and boil for an
additional 2 minutes. Let the
syrup cool completely.

2 Place one-third of all
the nuts in a food
processor and process until
finely chopped. Coarsely chop
the remainder. Place all the
chopped nuts in a bowl with
the sugar, cinnamon, and
nutmeg and mix together.

3 Grease a baking pan
that is roughly the same
size as, or slightly smaller than,

the sheets of pastry. Preheat
the oven to 350°F/180°C.
Brush 1 sheet of pastry with
butter and place on the
bottom of the baking pan.
Repeat with 3 more sheets.
Spread one-third of the nut
mixture over the pastry. Top
with 2 more layers of buttered
pastry, then another third of
the nut mixture. Top with
2 more buttered phyllo sheets,

then the remaining nuts.
Finally top with 4 sheets
of buttered phyllo.

4 Cut the top layer of
pastry into diamonds
and bake for 30–40 minutes, or
until crisp and golden. Remove
from the oven, pour the syrup
over the top, and cool. When
cold, trim the edges and cut
into diamond shapes.

lime & coconut meringue pie

serves 6　　　　**prep: 30 mins** ⏱　　　　**cook: 40–50 mins** 🍳

Rich coconut milk adds a Caribbean flavor to this variation on a traditional classic—ever-popular lemon meringue pie.

INGREDIENTS

butter, for greasing

all-purpose flour, for dusting

1 quantity Unsweetened Pie Dough

(see page 13)

FILLING

4 tbsp cornstarch

1¾ cups canned coconut milk

grated rind and juice of 2 limes

2 large eggs, separated

scant 1 cup superfine sugar

zest of 1 lime, to decorate

NUTRITIONAL INFORMATION

Calories 403

Protein 6g

Carbohydrate 66g

Sugars 35g

Fat 15g

Saturates 7g

variation

Add a teaspoon of coconut liqueur to the filling with the sugar in Step 2, if you like.

cook's tip

Be careful not to overcook the meringue, otherwise it will become hard and dry rather than soft and delicious.

1 Preheat the oven to 400°F/200°C, then grease a 9-inch/23-cm tart pan. On a lightly floured counter, roll out the pastry, and use it to line the tart pan, then bake blind (see page 13). Reduce the oven temperature to 325°F/160°C and place a cookie sheet in the oven.

2 To make the filling, place the cornstarch in a pan with a little of the coconut milk and stir to make a paste. Stir in the rest of the coconut milk. Bring to a boil slowly, stirring constantly. Cook over medium–high heat, stirring, for 3 minutes, or until thickened. Remove from the heat and add the lime rind and juice, the egg yolks, and ¼ cup of the superfine sugar. Pour into the pie shell.

3 Place the egg whites in a spotlessly clean, greasefree bowl and whisk until very stiff, then gradually whisk in the remaining superfine sugar. Spread the meringue over the filling and swirl with a spatula. Bake in the preheated oven for 20 minutes, or until lightly browned. Decorate with lime zest and serve hot or cold.

raspberry éclairs

makes 8   **prep: 30 mins** ⏲   **cook: 40 mins** ⏲

*These choux buns are perfect for serving as a dessert
or for an al fresco meal in high summer.*

INGREDIENTS

CHOUX PASTRY

2 oz/55 g butter

⅔ cup water

½ cup all-purpose flour, sifted

2 eggs, beaten

FILLING

1⅓ cups heavy cream

1 tbsp confectioners' sugar

¾ cup fresh raspberries

FROSTING

generous 1 cup confectioners' sugar

2 tsp lemon juice

pink food coloring (optional)

NUTRITIONAL INFORMATION

Calories 141

Protein 2g

Carbohydrate 10g

Sugars 8g

Fat 11g

Saturates 6g

variation

You could use other fresh summer
fruits, such as halved strawberries,
for these éclairs.

cook's tip

The raw choux mixture can be
made and shaped a few days
ahead and frozen, then baked
directly from the freezer for
5 minutes longer than usual.

1 Preheat the oven to 400°F/200°C. To make the choux pastry, place the butter and water in a large, heavy-bottom pan and bring to a boil. Add the flour, all at once, and beat thoroughly until the mixture leaves the sides of the pan. Let cool slightly, then vigorously beat in the eggs, 1 at a time.

2 Spoon the mixture into a pastry bag fitted with a ½-inch/1-cm nozzle and make 8 x 3-inch/7.5-cm lengths on several dampened cookie sheets. Bake in the oven for 30 minutes, or until crisp and golden. Remove from the oven and make a small hole in each éclair with the tip of a knife to let out the steam, then return to the oven for an additional 5 minutes, to dry out the insides. Transfer to a wire rack to cool.

3 To make the filling, place the cream and confectioners' sugar in a bowl and whisk until thick. Split the éclairs and fill with the cream and raspberries. To make the frosting, sift the confectioners' sugar into a bowl and stir in the lemon juice and enough water to make a smooth paste. Add pink food coloring, if desired. Drizzle the frosting generously over the éclairs, and let set before serving.

date & apricot tart

serves 8

prep: 15 mins, plus 30 mins chilling

cook: 50 mins

There is no need to add any extra sugar to this filling because the dry fruit is naturally sweet. This tart is suitable for vegans.

INGREDIENTS

1½ cups whole-wheat flour, plus extra for dusting

generous ¼ cup mixed nuts, ground

3½ oz/100 g vegan margarine, cut into small pieces

4 tbsp water

1⅓ cups no-soak dried apricots, chopped

1⅓ cups chopped stoned dates

scant 2 cups apple juice

1 tsp ground cinnamon

grated rind of 1 lemon

soy custard, to serve (optional)

NUTRITIONAL INFORMATION

Calories	.359
Protein	.7g
Carbohydrate	.53g
Sugars	.34g
Fat	.15g
Saturates	.2g

cook's tip

Just dampen the edge of the tart when fixing the decorative lattice on top, otherwise the pastry may become soggy.

1 Place the flour and ground nuts in a bowl, add the margarine and rub it in with your fingertips until the mixture resembles bread crumbs. Stir in the water and mix to form a dough. Cover and let chill for 30 minutes.

2 Preheat the oven to 400°F/200°C. Place the apricots and dates in a pan, together with the apple juice, cinnamon, and lemon rind. Bring to a boil, cover, and let simmer over low heat for 15 minutes, or until the fruit softens and can be mashed to a purée.

3 Set aside a small ball of pie dough for making lattice strips. Roll out the rest of the dough on a lightly floured counter to form a circle, then use to line a 9-inch/23-cm loose-bottom tart pan.

4 Spread the date and apricot filling evenly over the bottom of the pastry shell. Roll out the reserved dough on a lightly floured counter and cut into strips ½-inch/1-cm wide. Cut the strips to fit the tart and gently twist them across the top of the fruit to form a decorative lattice pattern. Moisten the edges of the strips with water and seal them firmly round the rim of the tart. Bake in the oven for 25–30 minutes, or until golden brown. Cut into slices and serve with soy custard, if you like.

one roll fruit pie

cook: 35 mins

prep: 15 mins, plus 30 mins chilling

serves 8

This is an easy way to make a pie, once you have rolled out the pie dough and filled it you just turn the edges of the pie dough in!

NUTRITIONAL INFORMATION

Calories 229

Protein 4g

Carbohydrate 30g

Sugars 13g

Fat 11g

Saturates 7g

INGREDIENTS

3½ oz/100 g butter, cut into small pieces, plus extra for greasing
1⅛ cups all-purpose flour, plus extra for dusting
1 tbsp water
1 egg, separated
sugar cubes, crushed, for sprinkling

FILLING

1 lb 5 oz/600 g prepared fruit, such as rhubarb, gooseberries, or plums
generous ⅓ cup brown sugar
1 tbsp ground ginger

cook's tip

If the pie dough breaks when shaping it into a circle, don't panic—just patch and seal, as the overall effect of this tart is rough.

1 Grease a large cookie sheet with a little butter. Place the flour and butter in a large bowl, add the butter and rub it in with your fingertips until the mixture resembles bread crumbs. Add the water and mix together to form a soft dough. Cover and let chill in the refrigerator for 30 minutes.

2 Preheat the oven to 400°F/200°C. Roll out the dough on a lightly floured counter, to a circle 14 inches/35 cm in diameter. Transfer the circle to the center of the cookie sheet and brush with the egg yolk.

3 To make the filling, mix the prepared fruit with the brown sugar and ground ginger and pile it into the center of the pie dough. Turn in the edges of the dough all the way round. Brush the surface of the dough with the egg white and sprinkle with the crushed sugar cubes.

4 Bake in the oven for 35 minutes, or until golden brown. Transfer to a serving plate and serve warm.

summer fruit tartlets

makes 12 **prep: 25 mins, plus** 🕐 **30 mins chilling** **cook: 12–18 mins** 🕐

Small almond pastry shells filled with bright summer fruits taste as good as they look, with their delicate combination of flavors.

INGREDIENTS

DOUGH

scant 1½ cups all-purpose flour, plus extra for dusting

generous ¾ cup confectioners' sugar

⅔ cup ground almonds

4 oz/115 g butter

1 egg yolk

1 tbsp milk

FILLING

1 cup cream cheese

confectioners' sugar, to taste, plus extra for dusting

12 oz/350 g fresh summer fruits, such as red and white currants, blueberries, raspberries, and small strawberries

variation

The fruit in the tarts could be brushed with warmed red currant jelly to make an attractive glaze.

cook's tip

If you wash the summer fruits just before using them, be sure to drain them well on paper towels, otherwise the liquid will make the tartlet cases soggy.

1 To make the dough, sift the flour and confectioners' sugar into a bowl. Stir in the ground almonds. Add the butter and rub in until the mixture resembles bread crumbs. Add the egg yolk and milk and work in with a spatula, then mix with your fingers until the dough binds together. Wrap the dough in plastic wrap and let chill in the refrigerator for 30 minutes.

2 Preheat the oven to 400°F/200°C. On a floured counter, roll out the dough and use to line 12 deep tartlet or individual brioche pans. Prick the bottoms. Press a piece of foil into each tartlet, covering the edges, and bake in the preheated oven for 10–15 minutes, or until light golden brown. Remove the foil and bake for an additional 2–3 minutes. Transfer to a wire rack to cool.

3 To make the filling, place the cream cheese and confectioners' sugar in a bowl and mix together. Place a spoonful of filling in each tart shell and arrange the fruit on top. Dust with sifted confectioners' sugar and serve.

pear & pecan strudel

serves 4   **prep: 15 mins**   **cook: 30–35 mins**

Crisp phyllo pastry is wrapped round a nutty pear filling in this easy-to-make strudel for a traditional, but unusual, dessert.

INGREDIENTS

2 ripe pears

2 oz/55 g butter, plus extra,
melted, for brushing

1 cup fresh white bread crumbs

generous ½ cup chopped pecans

2 tbsp brown sugar

finely grated rind of 1 orange

3½ oz/100 g ready-made phyllo pastry

scant ¼ cup orange blossom honey

2 tbsp orange juice

confectioners' sugar, for dusting

strained plain yogurt, to serve

NUTRITIONAL INFORMATION

Calories	.466
Protein	.6g
Carbohydrate	.52g
Sugars	.30g
Fat	.28g
Saturates	.9g

cook's tip

When working with phyllo pastry, it is important to keep it covered until you are ready to use it, otherwise it will dry out very quickly.

1 Preheat the oven to 400°F/200°C. Peel, core, and chop the pears. Place 1 tablespoon of the butter in a skillet over low heat, add the bread crumbs, and gently cook until golden. Transfer the bread crumbs to a bowl and add the chopped pears with the nuts, sugar, and orange rind. Place the remaining butter in a small pan and heat until melted.

2 Keep 1 sheet of phyllo pastry back, keeping it well wrapped, and layer the remaining phyllo sheets on a clean counter, brushing each one with a little melted butter. Spoon the nut filling onto the phyllo sheets, leaving a 1-inch/ 2.5-cm margin round the edges. Drizzle with the honey and orange juice.

3 Fold the short ends over the filling, then roll up, starting at a long side. Lift onto a cookie sheet, seam-side up. Brush with any remaining melted butter and crumple the remaining sheet of phyllo pastry round the strudel. Bake in the oven for 25 minutes, or until golden and crisp. Dust with sifted confectioners' sugar and serve warm with strained plain yogurt.

sicilian ricotta tart

 cook: 1 hr 25 mins–
 1 hr 40 mins

 prep: 15 mins

serves 6

Pine nuts and candied peel are included in the filling of this Italian specialty. It makes a perfect dinner party dessert.

NUTRITIONAL INFORMATION	
Calories 207	
Protein 8g	
Carbohydrate 16g	
Sugars 16g	
Fat 13g	
Saturates 4g	

INGREDIENTS

butter, for greasing

all-purpose flour, for dusting

1 quantity Pâte Sucrée (see page 13)

FILLING

scant 1¼ cups ricotta cheese

2 eggs, beaten

¼ cup golden superfine sugar

scant ½ cup pine nuts

generous ⅓ cup chopped candied peel

finely grated rind of 1 lemon

½ tsp vanilla extract

confectioners' sugar, for dusting

cook's tip

If possible, it is best to buy packages of whole pieces of candied peel, if your local food store stocks them, and chop them up yourself.

1 Preheat the oven to 400°F/200°C, then grease an 8-inch/20-cm tart pan. On a lightly floured counter, roll out the pastry and use it to line the pan, then bake blind (see page 13). Reduce the oven temperature to 350°F/180°C and place a cookie sheet in the oven.

2 To make the filling, press the ricotta cheese through a strainer into a bowl. Add the eggs, sugar, pine nuts, candied peel, lemon rind, and vanilla extract. Mix well, then pour into the tart shell.

3 Place the tart on the preheated cookie sheet and bake in the preheated oven for 45 minutes, or until lightly set. Let cool, then dust with sifted confectioners' sugar and serve.

chocolate, chestnut & ginger tart

serves 8   **prep: 30 mins, plus ⏲ 1–2 hrs chilling**   **cook: 45 mins ⏲**

The cookie-crumb tart shell used in this recipe is ideal if you do not want to go to the trouble of making dough.

INGREDIENTS

COOKIE SHELL	2 eggs
6 tbsp butter	3½ oz/100 g semisweet
9 oz/250 g ginger cookies, crushed	chocolate, melted
	2 oz/55 g candied ginger, cut into
FILLING	tiny slivers
6 oz/175 g unsweetened	¼ cup ground almonds
chestnut purée	
¼ cup golden superfine sugar	TO DECORATE
generous ¾ cup ricotta cheese	⅔ cup whipping cream
	chocolate curls

NUTRITIONAL INFORMATION

Calories	.509
Protein	.8g
Carbohydrate	.53g
Sugars	.32g
Fat	.31g
Saturates	.17g

variations

Substitute the chocolate decoration with slivers of candied ginger or a sprinkling of ground ginger mixed with sweet drinking chocolate powder.

cook's tip

You can use other types of cookies or crackers to make a shell for a tart, such as graham crackers. To work well, the crackers need to be fairly rich and buttery.

1 Preheat the oven to 350°F/180°C. Place the butter in a pan over low heat until just melted. Stir in the crushed cookies. Press the crumbs onto the bottom and up the sides of a 9-inch/23-cm loose-bottom tart pan. Bake in the preheated oven for 10 minutes, then let cool. Leave the oven switched on.

2 To make the filling, place the chestnut purée and sugar in a bowl and beat until smooth. Place the ricotta cheese and eggs in a separate bowl and beat until smooth. Carefully stir the melted chocolate into the ricotta mixture. Add the chestnut purée mixture and mix thoroughly. Stir in the ginger and ground almonds.

3 Pour the filling into the tart shell and bake in the preheated oven for 35 minutes, or until it is lightly set. Let cool, then chill in the refrigerator for 1–2 hours.

4 Before serving, place the cream in a bowl and whip until thick. Spread over the top of the tart and sprinkle with chocolate curls.

maple pecan tarts

makes 12

prep: 20 mins, plus 10–30 mins cooling

cook: 20–25 mins

Rich maple syrup and pecans give a wonderful flavor to the toffee filling in these moreish little tarts.

INGREDIENTS

DOUGH	FILLING
1 cup all-purpose flour, plus extra for dusting	2 tbsp maple syrup
6 tbsp butter	⅔ cup heavy cream
¼ cup golden superfine sugar	generous ½ cup golden superfine sugar
2 egg yolks	pinch of cream of tartar
	scant ⅓ cup water
	1 cup pecans
	12 pecan nut halves, to decorate

variation

Pipe whipped cream round the edges of the cooled tarts for a more decorative presentation.

cook's tip

It is important to use genuine maple syrup rather than the readily-available maple-flavored syrup, to make sure that the tarts are rich and flavorsome.

1 Sift the flour into a large bowl, then cut the butter into pieces and rub it into the flour using your fingertips until the mixture resembles bread crumbs. Stir in the sugar, then stir in the egg yolks to make a smooth dough. Wrap in plastic wrap and chill in the refrigerator for 30 minutes.

2 Preheat the oven to 400°F/200°C. On a floured counter, roll out the pastry thinly, cut out circles, and use to line 12 tartlet pans. Prick the bottoms and press a piece of foil into each tart shell. Bake in the oven for 10–15 minutes, or until light golden. Remove the foil and bake for a further 2–3 minutes. Let cool on a wire rack.

3 To make the filling, place half the maple syrup and half the cream in a bowl and mix together. Place the sugar, cream of tartar, and water in a pan over low heat and stir until the sugar dissolves. Bring to a boil and continue boiling until light golden. Remove from the heat and stir in the maple syrup and cream mixture.

4 Return to the heat and cook to the "soft ball" stage (240°F/116°C), when a little of the mixture forms a soft ball when dropped into cold water. Stir in the remaining cream and let stand until warm. Brush the remaining syrup over the edges of the tarts. Place the pecans in the shells, spoon in the toffee and top with a nut half. Let cool.

crab & ginger triangles

makes 12 **prep: 15–20 mins** **cook: 20–25 mins**

These crisp little crab pockets could be served as an unusual appetizer at a dinner party, or as a snack at a buffet or with drinks.

INGREDIENTS

6 tbsp butter, melted, plus
extra for greasing
7 oz/200 g fresh or canned
crabmeat, drained
6 scallions, finely chopped,
plus extra to garnish
1-inch/2.5-cm piece of fresh gingerroot,
peeled and grated
2 tsp soy sauce
pepper
12 sheets ready-made phyllo pastry

NUTRITIONAL INFORMATION

Calories	.105
Protein	.4g
Carbohydrate	.8g
Sugars	.1g
Fat	.6g
Saturates	.4g

cook's tip

It is a good idea to use fresh crabmeat for this recipe, if it is available, instead of less flavorsome canned crabmeat.

1 Preheat the oven to 350°F/180°C, then grease a cookie sheet. Place the crabmeat, scallions, ginger, and soy sauce in a bowl, add pepper to taste, mix together, and reserve. Working with 1 sheet of phyllo pastry at a time and keeping the rest covered with a cloth, brush a pastry sheet with melted butter, fold in half lengthwise and brush again with butter.

2 Place a spoonful of the crab mixture in one corner of the pastry strip. Fold the pastry and filling over at right angles to make a triangle enclosing the filling. Continue folding in this way all the way down the strip to make a triangular pocket.

3 Place the pocket on the prepared cookie sheet. Repeat with the remaining pastry and crab mixture. Brush each parcel with melted butter. Bake in the preheated oven for 20–25 minutes, or until crisp and golden brown. Garnish with extra chopped scallions and serve warm.

phyllo tartlets with avocado salsa

cook: 6–8 mins   **prep: 20 mins**   **makes 20**

Phyllo pastry makes crisp little containers for a spicy avocado salsa.
If you are making these for a party, fill them just before serving.

NUTRITIONAL INFORMATION

Calories	49
Protein	. . . . .1g
Carbohydrate	. . . . .3g
Sugars	. . . . .1g
Fat	. . . . .4g
Saturates	. . . . .2g

INGREDIENTS

TARTLET SHELLS

2½ oz/70 g ready-made phyllo pastry

3 tbsp melted butter, plus

extra for greasing

AVOCADO SALSA

1 large avocado

1 small red onion, finely chopped

1 fresh chile, seeded and

finely chopped

2 tomatoes, peeled, seeded, and

finely chopped

juice of 1 lime

2 tbsp chopped fresh cilantro

salt and pepper

cook's tip

The tartlet shells can be made up to a week in advance and stored in an airtight container. Make the salsa just before serving. When the shells are filled, serve them straight away, otherwise they will go soft.

1 Preheat the oven to 350°F/180°C. To make the tartlet shells, working with 1 sheet of phyllo pastry at a time and keeping the rest covered with a cloth, brush the pastry sheet with melted butter. With a sharp knife, cut the sheet into 2-inch/5-cm squares.

2 Grease 20 cups in mini muffin pans and line each one with 3 buttered phyllo pastry squares, setting each one at an angle to the others. Repeat until all the pastry is used up. Bake in the preheated oven for 6–8 minutes, or until crisp and golden. Carefully transfer to a wire rack to cool.

3 To make the salsa, peel the avocado and remove the stone. Cut the flesh into small cubes and place in a bowl with the onion, chile, tomatoes, lime juice, and cilantro, and add salt and pepper to taste. Divide the avocado salsa between the tartlet shells and serve immediately.

mini choux puffs with shrimp cocktail

makes 22   **prep: 30 mins** ⏲   **cook: 35 mins** ⏱

Shrimp cocktail is making a comeback, but here it is given a new look, served in mini choux pastries as a cocktail snack.

INGREDIENTS

CHOUX PASTRY	FILLING
2 oz/55 g butter, plus extra for greasing	2 tbsp mayonnaise
⅔ cup water	1 tsp tomato paste
½ cup all-purpose flour, sifted	5 oz/140 g small shrimp, cooked and peeled
2 eggs, beaten	1 tsp Worcestershire sauce
	salt
	Tabasco sauce
	1 Boston lettuce, shredded
	cayenne pepper, to garnish

NUTRITIONAL INFORMATION

Calories	.65
Protein	.3g
Carbohydrate	.3g
Sugars	.0g
Fat	.5g
Saturates	.2g

variation

If you prefer, garnish with thin slivers of red bell pepper instead of the cayenne pepper.

cook's tip

The choux puffs can be filled up to 3 hours in advance, then chilled in the refrigerator until you are ready to serve them. Bring them to room temperature before serving.

1 Preheat the oven to 350°F/180°C, then grease a cookie sheet. To make the choux pastry, place the butter and water in a large, heavy-bottom pan and bring to a boil. Add the flour, all at once, and beat thoroughly until the mixture leaves the sides of the pan. Let cool slightly, then vigorously beat in the eggs, 1 at a time. Place 22 walnut-size spoonfuls of the mixture onto the cookie sheet, spaced ¾ inch/2 cm apart. Bake in the preheated oven for 35 minutes, or until light, crisp, and golden. Transfer to a wire rack to cool, then cut a ¼-inch/5-mm slice from the top of each puff.

2 To make the filling, place the mayonnaise, tomato paste, shrimp, and Worcestershire sauce in a bowl. Add salt and Tabasco sauce to taste, and mix together until combined.

3 Place a few lettuce shreds in the bottom of each puff, making sure some protrude at the top. Spoon the shrimp mixture on top and dust with a little cayenne pepper before serving.

greek feta & olive tartlets

makes 12 **prep: 30 mins** **cook: 30 mins**

Tangy feta cheese and fruity olives make a tasty filling for these baby quiches, which are ideal for party buffets.

INGREDIENTS

butter, for greasing
all-purpose flour, for dusting
1 quantity Unsweetened Pie Dough
(see page 13)
1 egg
3 egg yolks
1¼ cups whipping cream
salt and pepper
4 oz/115 g feta cheese
6 pitted black olives, halved
12 small fresh rosemary sprigs

NUTRITIONAL INFORMATION

Calories	208
Protein	. . . . .4g
Carbohydrate	. . . . .8g
Sugars	. . . . .1g
Fat	. . . . .18g
Saturates	. . . . .9g

cook's tip

Feta cheese is quite salty so there is no need to add much extra salt when you season the egg mixture in Step 2.

1 Preheat the oven to 400°F/200°C. Grease 12 individual 2½-inch/6-cm tart pans, or the cups in a 12-hole muffin pan. On a floured counter, roll out the pastry to ⅛ inch/3 mm thick. Use to line the prepared pans and prick the bottoms with a fork. Press a square of foil into each tartlet shell and bake in the preheated oven

for 12 minutes. Remove the foil and bake for an additional 3 minutes.

2 Place the egg, egg yolks, and cream in a bowl, add salt and pepper to taste, and beat together.

3 Crumble the feta cheese into the tartlet shells and spoon over the egg

mixture. Place half an olive and a rosemary sprig on top of each tartlet, then bake in the oven for 15 minutes, or until the filling is just set. Serve warm or cold.

instant pesto & goat cheese tartlets

cook: 10 mins   **prep: 15 mins**   **makes 20**

*The puff pastry in these tartlets rises up round the flavorsome filling
to make an instant tartlet shell!*

NUTRITIONAL INFORMATION

Calories	66
Protein	2g
Carbohydrate	4g
Sugars	1g
Fat	5g
Saturates	1g

INGREDIENTS

7 oz/200 g ready-made puff pastry

all-purpose flour, for dusting

3 tbsp pesto

20 cherry tomatoes, each cut
into 3 slices

4 oz/115 g goat cheese

salt and pepper

fresh basil sprigs, to garnish

1 Preheat the oven
to 400°F/200°C, then
lightly flour a cookie sheet.
Roll out the pastry on a floured
counter to ⅛ inch/3 mm thick.
Cut out 20 circles with a
2-inch/5-cm plain cutter and
arrange the pastry circles on
the floured cookie sheet.

2 Spread a little pesto on
each circle, leaving a
margin round the edges, then
arrange 3 tomato slices on top
of each one.

3 Crumble the goat
cheese over and season
to taste with salt and pepper.
Bake in the preheated oven for
10 minutes, or until the pastry
is puffed up, crisp, and golden.
Garnish with basil sprigs and
serve warm.

cook's tip

These tartlets are even quicker
to make if you use the ready-
rolled variety of ready-made
puff pastry, which is available
in most large food stores.

onion & mozzarella tarts

serves 4 **prep: 20 mins, plus 40 mins chilling** **cook: 45 mins**

These individual tarts are delicious hot or cold, are great for lunch boxes or picnics and make a good dinner party appetizer.

INGREDIENTS

9 oz/250 g package puff pastry, thawed if frozen

all-purpose flour, for dusting

2 red onions

1 red bell pepper

8 cherry tomatoes, halved

3½ oz/100 g mozzarella cheese, cut into chunks

8 fresh thyme sprigs

NUTRITIONAL INFORMATION

Calories 327

Protein 5g

Carbohydrate 25g

Sugars 3g

Fat 23g

Saturates 9g

cook's tip

Ready-made puff pastry is usually sold either chilled or frozen in most stores. If using frozen, make sure it is thoroughly thawed.

1 Roll out the pastry on a lightly floured counter until large enought to cut out 4 x 3-inch/7.5-cm squares. Using a sharp knife, trim the edges of the pastry, reserving the trimmings. Let the pastry chill in the refrigerator for 30 minutes.

2 Preheat the oven to 400°F/200°C and preheat the broiler. Place the pastry squares on a cookie sheet. Brush a little water along each edge of the pastry squares and use the reserved pastry trimmings to make a rim round each tart. Cut the red onions into thin wedges and halve and seed the bell pepper.

3 Place the onions and bell pepper in a roasting pan and cook under the broiler for 15 minutes, or until charred. Place the roasted bell pepper in a plastic bag and let sweat for 10 minutes. When the bell pepper is cool enough to handle, peel off the skin and cut the flesh into strips.

4 Line the pastry squares with squares of foil and bake in the preheated oven for 10 minutes. Remove and discard the foil squares and bake the tart shells for an additional 5 minutes.

5 Place the onions, bell pepper strips, tomatoes, and cheese in each tart and sprinkle with the fresh thyme. Return to the oven for 15 minutes, or until the pastry is golden. Serve hot or cold.

cheese & onion pies

cook: 35 mins   **prep: 10 mins**   **serves 4**

These crisp pies are filled with a tasty onion, garlic, and parsley mixture, making them ideal for lunch boxes.

NUTRITIONAL INFORMATION

Calories	.544
Protein	.11g
Carbohydrate	.47g
Sugars	.9g
Fat	.36g
Saturates	.18g

INGREDIENTS

3 tbsp vegetable oil

4 onions, thinly sliced

4 garlic cloves, crushed

4 tbsp finely chopped fresh parsley

generous ⅝ cup sharp cheese, grated

salt and pepper

PIE DOUGH

1⅛ cups all-purpose flour

½ tsp salt

3½ oz/100 g butter, cut into
small pieces

3–4 tbsp water

cook's tip

You can prepare the onion filling in advance and store it in the refrigerator until required. Return it to room temperature before using.

1 Preheat the oven to 425°F/220°C. Heat the oil in a skillet. Add the onions and garlic and cook for 10–15 minutes, or until the onion is soft. Remove the skillet from the heat and stir in the parsley and cheese. Season to taste with salt and pepper.

2 To make the pie dough, sift the flour and salt into a large bowl. Add the butter and rub it in with your fingertips until the mixture resembles fine bread crumbs. Gradually stir in the water and mix to form a dough.

3 Roll out the dough on a lightly floured counter, and divide it into 8 portions. Roll out each portion to a 4-inch/10-cm circle and use half of the circles to line 4 individual tart pans. Fill each circle with a quarter of the cheese and onion mixture. Cover with the remaining 4 pastry circles. Make a slit in the top of each tart with the tip of a knife to allow steam to escape during cooking and seal the edges of the pies with the back of a teaspoon. Bake in the preheated oven for 20 minutes. Serve the tarts hot or cold.

chicken bake

⏲ **cook: 40 mins**   ⏲ **prep: 45 mins, plus 1 hr cooling**   **serves 4**

NUTRITIONAL INFORMATION

Calories 530

Protein 37g

Carbohydrate 48g

Sugars 8g

Fat 23g

Saturates 12g

This recipe is a type of cottage pie and is just as versatile. Add vegetables and herbs of your choice, depending on what you have at hand.

INGREDIENTS

2¼ cups ground chicken

1 large onion, finely chopped

2 carrots, finely diced

2 tbsp all-purpose flour

1 tbsp tomato paste

1¼ cups chicken stock

salt and pepper

pinch of fresh thyme

2 lb/900 g boiled potatoes, creamed with butter and milk and highly seasoned

¾ cup grated Jack cheese

freshly cooked peas, to serve

variation

Instead of Jack cheese, you could use a mixture of cheeses, depending on what you have available.

cook's tip

Make sure that the filling is piping hot before serving. If time is limited you can cook the chicken bake in the oven without letting it cool down.

1 Dry-fry the ground chicken, onion, and carrots in a large, nonstick pan over low heat, stirring frequently, for 5 minutes, or until the chicken has lost its pink color. Sprinkle the chicken with the flour and cook, stirring constantly, for an additional 2 minutes.

2 Gradually blend in the tomato paste and stock, then let simmer for 15 minutes. Season to taste with salt and pepper and add the thyme.

3 Transfer the chicken and vegetable mixture to a large casserole and let cool completely.

4 Preheat the oven to 400°F/200°C. Spoon the creamed potato over the chicken mixture and sprinkle with the Jack cheese. Bake in the preheated oven for 20 minutes, or until the cheese is bubbling and golden, then serve with freshly cooked peas.

chicken lasagna

serves 4   prep: 20 mins ⏲   cook: 1 hr 15 mins ⏲

This variation of the traditional beef dish has layers of pasta and chicken or turkey baked in red wine, tomatoes, and a delicious rich cheese sauce. Serve with a crisp salad for a filling supper dish.

INGREDIENTS

9 sheets fresh or dried lasagna

salt and pepper

1 tbsp olive oil, plus extra for oiling

1 red onion, finely chopped

1 garlic clove, crushed

3½ oz/100 g mushrooms, sliced

12 oz/350 g chicken or turkey breast, cut into chunks

⅔ cup red wine, diluted with generous ⅓ cup water

9 oz/250 g strained tomatoes

1 tsp sugar

Parmesan cheese, for sprinkling

BECHAMEL SAUCE

5 tbsp butter

5 tbsp all-purpose flour

2½ cups milk

1 egg, beaten

scant ¾ cup Parmesan cheese, finely grated

NUTRITIONAL INFORMATION

Calories	.550
Protein	.35g
Carbohydrate	.34g
Sugars	.11g
Fat	.29g
Saturates	.12g

variation

Replace the Parmesan cheese with another hard cheese, such as Cheddar, if you prefer. Use spinach-flavored lasagna sheets, if you like.

cook's tip

If your time is very limited, use no-precook lasagna sheets, which are usually available from most large supermarkets or Italian delicatessens.

1 Preheat the oven to 375°F/190°C. Bring a large pan of lightly salted water to a boil. Add the lasagna sheets and cook according to the package instructions. Lightly oil a deep ovenproof dish.

2 Heat the olive oil in a skillet. Add the onion and garlic and cook for 3–4 minutes. Add the mushrooms and chicken and stir-fry for 4 minutes, or until the meat is brown. Add the wine, bring to a boil, then lower the heat and let simmer for 5 minutes. Stir in the strained tomatoes and sugar and cook for 3–5 minutes, until the meat is cooked. The sauce should have thickened, but still be quite runny.

3 To make the sauce, melt the butter in a pan, stir in the flour, and cook for 2 minutes. Remove the pan from the heat and gradually add the milk, mixing to form a smooth sauce. Return to the heat and bring to a boil, stirring until thickened. Cool slightly, then beat in the egg and half of the cheese. Season to taste.

4 Place 3 sheets of lasagna in the bottom of the prepared dish and spread with half of the chicken mixture. Repeat the layers. Top with the last 3 sheets of lasagna, pour over the sauce and sprinkle with the grated Parmesan cheese. Bake in the oven for 30 minutes, or until golden and cooked through.

turkey & vegetable loaf

serves 6 **prep: 10 mins** **cook: 1 hr 20 mins**

This impressive-looking turkey loaf is flavored with herbs and a layer of juicy tomatoes and covered with zucchini ribbons.

INGREDIENTS

1 onion, finely chopped

1 garlic clove, crushed

2 lb/900 g lean ground turkey

1 tbsp chopped fresh parsley

1 tbsp chopped fresh chives

1 tbsp chopped fresh tarragon

salt and pepper

1 egg white, lightly beaten

2 zucchinis, 1 medium, 1 large

2 tomatoes

tomato and herb sauce, to serve

(optional)

NUTRITIONAL INFORMATION

Calories	165
Protein	. . . . .36g
Carbohydrate	. . . . .1g
Sugars	. . . . .1g
Fat	. . . . .2g
Saturates	. . . . .0.5g

cook's tip

To test if the loaf is cooked, insert a skewer into the center —the juices should run clear. The loaf will also shrink away from the sides of the pan.

1 Preheat the oven to 375°F/190°C. Line a nonstick loaf pan with parchment paper. Place the onion, garlic, and turkey in a bowl, add the herbs and season to taste with salt and pepper. Mix together with your hands, then add the egg white to bind.

2 Press half of the turkey mixture into the bottom of the pan. Thinly slice the medium zucchini and the tomatoes and arrange the slices over the meat. Top with the rest of the turkey mixture and press down. Cover with foil and place in a roasting pan. Pour in enough boiling water to come halfway up the sides of the loaf pan. Bake in

the oven for 1–1¼ hours, removing the foil for the last 20 minutes of cooking.

3 Cut the zucchini lengthwise into thin slices with a vegetable peeler or metal cheese slice. Bring a pan of water to a boil and blanch the zucchini for 1–2 minutes, or until just tender. Drain and keep warm.

4 Remove the turkey loaf from the pan and transfer to a warmed serving platter. Drape the zucchini ribbons over the turkey loaf and serve with a tomato and herb sauce, if you like.

mini cheese & onion tarts

cook: 25 mins

prep: 45 mins, plus 30 mins chilling

serves 12

Serve these delicious little savory tarts as finger food at buffets or drinks parties. They are also excellent for picnics.

NUTRITIONAL INFORMATION

Calories	114
Protein	3g
Carbohydrate	7g
Sugars	1g
Fat	9g
Saturates	5g

INGREDIENTS

PIE DOUGH

⅔ cup all-purpose flour, plus extra for dusting

¼ tsp salt

5½ tbsp butter, cut into small pieces

1–2 tbsp water

FILLING

1 egg, beaten

generous ⅓ cup light cream

generous ⅜ cup Jack cheese, grated

3 scallions, finely chopped

salt

cayenne pepper

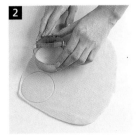

cook's tip

If you use 6 oz/175 g of ready-made unsweetened pie dough instead of making it yourself, these tarts can be made in the matter of minutes.

1 To make the pie dough, sift the flour and salt into a large bowl. Add the butter and rub it in with your fingertips until the mixture resembles bread crumbs. Stir in the water and mix to form a dough. Form the dough into a ball, cover with plastic wrap, and let chill in the refrigerator for 30 minutes.

2 Preheat the oven to 350°F/180°C. Roll out the pie dough on a lightly floured counter. Using a 3-inch/7.5-cm cookie cutter, stamp out 12 circles from the dough and line a tartlet pan.

3 To make the filling, whisk the beaten egg, cream, grated cheese, and scallions together in a measuring cup. Season to taste with salt and cayenne pepper. Carefully pour the filling mixture into the pastry shells and bake in the preheated oven for 20–25 minutes, or until the filling is just set and the pastry is golden brown. Serve warm or cold.

smoky fish pie

cook: 1 hr   **prep: 15 mins**   **serves 4**

This flavorsome and colorful fish pie is perfect for a light supper. The addition of smoked salmon gives it a touch of luxury.

INGREDIENTS

2 lb/900 g smoked haddock or cod fillets	1 lb 8 oz/675 g potatoes, diced
2½ cups skim milk	5 tbsp lowfat plain yogurt
2 bay leaves	4 tbsp chopped fresh parsley
4 oz/115 g white mushrooms, quartered	salt and pepper
1 cup frozen peas	2 oz/55 g smoked salmon, sliced into thin strips
1 cup frozen corn kernels	3 tbsp cornstarch
	¼ cup smoked cheese, grated

variation

Substitute the white mushrooms with the same amount of cremini mushrooms, if you prefer.

cook's tip

If possible, use smoked haddock or cod that has not been dyed bright yellow or artificially flavored to give the illusion of having been smoked.

1 Preheat the oven to 400°F/200°C. Place the fish in a large, wide pan and add the milk and bay leaves. Bring to a boil, cover, and let simmer for 5 minutes. Add the mushrooms, peas, and corn, return to a simmer, cover, and cook for 5–7 minutes. Let cool.

2 Place the potatoes in a pan, cover with water, bring to a boil, and cook for 8 minutes. Drain well and mash. Stir in the yogurt, parsley, and season to taste with salt and pepper. Set aside.

3 Using a slotted spoon, remove the fish from the pan. Flake the fish away from the skin and place in an ovenproof gratin dish. Set aside the cooking liquid. Drain the vegetables, reserving the cooking liquid, and gently stir into the fish with the salmon strips.

4 Blend a little cooking liquid into the cornstarch to make a paste. Transfer the rest of the liquid to a pan and add the paste. Heat through, stirring, until thickened. Discard the bay leaves and season to taste with salt and pepper. Pour the sauce over the fish and vegetables and mix. Spoon over the mashed potato so that the fish is covered, sprinkle with cheese and bake in the oven for 25–30 minutes, or until the cheese is golden and bubbling.

fresh tomato tarts

serves 6

prep: 15 mins, plus 20 mins chilling

cook: 20 mins

These tomato-flavored tarts should be eaten as fresh as possible to enjoy the flaky and crisp buttery puff pastry.

INGREDIENTS

9 oz/250 g ready-made puff pastry, thawed if frozen

all-purpose flour, for dusting

1 egg, beaten

2 tbsp pesto

6 plum tomatoes, sliced

salt and pepper

fresh thyme leaves, to garnish (optional)

NUTRITIONAL INFORMATION

Calories	217
Protein	. . . . .5g
Carbohydrate	. . . . .18g
Sugars	. . . . .3g
Fat	. . . . .14g
Saturates	. . . . .1g

variation

Instead of individual tarts, roll the pastry out to form 1 large rectangle. Spoon over the pesto and arrange the tomatoes over the top.

1 Roll out the pastry on a lightly floured counter, to a rectangle measuring 12 x 10 inches/ 30 x 25 cm. Cut the rectangle in half and divide each half into 3 pieces to make 6 even-size rectangles. Let chill in the refrigerator for 20 minutes.

2 Preheat the oven to 400°F/200°C. Lightly score the edges of the pastry rectangles and brush them with the beaten egg. Spread the pesto over the rectangles, dividing it equally between them, leaving a 1-inch/2.5-cm border round each one. Arrange the tomato slices along the center of each rectangle on top of the pesto.

Season to taste with salt and pepper and lightly sprinkle with thyme leaves (if using).

3 Bake in the preheated oven for 15–20 minutes, or until well risen and golden brown. Transfer the tarts to warmed serving plates and serve while they are still piping hot.

provençal tart

cook: 55 mins

prep: 15 mins, plus 20 mins chilling

serves 6

This tart is full of color and flavor from the zucchinis and red and green bell peppers. It makes a great change from a quiche Lorraine.

NUTRITIONAL INFORMATION

Calories 355

Protein 5g

Carbohydrate 21g

Sugars 5g

Fat 29g

Saturates 9g

INGREDIENTS

9 oz/250 g ready-made puff pastry, thawed if frozen

all-purpose flour, for dusting

3 tbsp olive oil

2 red bell peppers, seeded and diced

2 green bell peppers, seeded and diced

⅔ cup heavy cream

1 egg

salt and pepper

2 zucchinis, sliced

cook's tip

This recipe could be used to make 6 individual tarts—use 6 x 4-inch/15 x 10-cm pans and bake them in the oven for 20 minutes, or until just set and golden brown.

1 Roll out the pastry on a lightly floured counter and use to line an 8-inch/20-cm loose-bottom tart pan. Let chill in the refrigerator for 20 minutes.

2 Preheat the oven to 350°F/180°C. Heat 2 tablespoons of the olive oil in a skillet and cook the bell peppers over low heat for 8 minutes, or until softened, stirring frequently. Whisk the heavy cream and egg together in a bowl and season to taste with salt and pepper. Stir in the bell peppers.

3 Heat the remaining oil in a separate skillet and cook the zucchini slices over medium heat, stirring frequently, for 4–5 minutes until lightly browned. Pour the egg and bell pepper mixture into the pastry shell. Arrange the courgette slices round the edge of the tart.

4 Bake in the preheated oven for 35–40 minutes, or until just set and golden brown. Serve immediately or cool in the pan.

ham & cheese lattice pies

serves 6

prep: 20 mins, plus 30 mins chilling

cook: 20 mins

These pretty lattice pies are equally delicious served hot or cold. They make a good picnic food served with salad.

INGREDIENTS

butter, for greasing

9 oz/250 g ready-made puff pastry, thawed if frozen

all-purpose flour, for dusting

1¾ oz/50 g ham, finely chopped

generous ½ cup whole soft cheese

2 tbsp snipped fresh chives

1 egg, beaten

generous ¼ cup Parmesan cheese, finely grated

pepper

NUTRITIONAL INFORMATION

Calories	.257
Protein	.8g
Carbohydrate	.16g
Sugars	.1g
Fat	.19g
Saturates	.5g

cook's tip

These pies can be made in advance, frozen uncooked, and baked fresh when required. Make sure that they are piping hot before serving.

1 Grease several cookie sheets. Roll out the pastry thinly on a lightly floured counter. Cut out 12 rectangles, each measuring 6 x 2 inches/15 x 5 cm. Place the rectangles on the prepared cookie sheets and let chill in the refrigerator for 30 minutes.

2 Preheat the oven to 350°F/180°C. Mix the ham, soft cheese, and chives together in a small bowl. Season with pepper to taste. Spread the ham, cheese, and chives mixture along the center of 6 of the rectangles, leaving a 1-inch/2.5-cm border round each one. Brush the border with the beaten egg.

3 To make the lattice pattern, fold the remaining rectangles lengthwise. Leaving a 1-inch/2.5-cm border, cut vertical lines across the folded edge of the pastry rectangles. Unfold the latticed rectangles and place them over the rectangles topped with the ham and cheese mixture on the cookie sheets. Seal the pastry edges well and lightly sprinkle the pies with the Parmesan cheese. Bake in the oven for 15–20 minutes. Serve hot or cold.

red onion tarte tatin

cook: 50 mins   **prep: 15 mins, plus 10 mins standing**   **serves 4**

Ready-made puff pastry works extremely well in this recipe and means you create a wonderful savory tart in very little time.

NUTRITIONAL INFORMATION

Calories 398

Protein 5g

Carbohydrate 40g

Sugars 14g

Fat 25g

Saturates 7g

INGREDIENTS

4 tbsp butter

6 tsp sugar

1 lb 2 oz/500 g red onions, quartered

3 tbsp red wine vinegar

2 tbsp fresh thyme leaves

salt and pepper

9 oz/250 g ready-made puff pastry, thawed if frozen

all-purpose flour, for dusting

variation

Replace the red onions with shallots, leaving them whole, if you prefer.

1 Preheat the oven to 350°F/180°C. Place the butter and sugar in a 9-inch/23-cm ovenproof skillet and cook over medium heat until melted and combined. Add the red onion quarters and sweat them over low heat, stirring occasionally, for 10–15 minutes, or until golden and caramelized.

2 Add the red wine vinegar and thyme leaves to the skillet. Season to taste with salt and pepper, then let simmer over medium heat until the liquid has reduced and the onion is coated in the buttery sauce.

3 Roll out the pastry on a lightly floured counter to a circle slightly larger than the skillet. Place the pastry over the onion mixture and press down, tucking in the edges to seal it.

4 Bake in the oven for 20–25 minutes, or until the pastry is firm and golden brown. Remove from the oven and let stand for 10 minutes. To turn out, place a serving plate over the skillet and, holding them firmly together, carefully invert them both so that the pastry becomes the bottom of the tart. Serve the tart warm.

beef & tomato gratin

serves 4   **prep: 10 mins** ⏱   **cook: 1 hr 15 mins** ⏱

A satisfying bake of lean ground beef, zucchinis, and tomatoes cooked in a lowfat "custard" with a cheesy crust.

INGREDIENTS

1½ cups lean ground beef

1 large onion, finely chopped

1 tsp dried mixed herbs

1 tbsp all-purpose flour

1¼ cups beef stock

1 tbsp tomato paste

salt and pepper

2 large tomatoes, thinly sliced

4 zucchinis, thinly sliced

2 tbsp cornstarch

1¼ cups skim milk

⅔ cup lowfat mascarpone cheese

1 egg yolk

⅝ cup freshly grated
Parmesan cheese

TO SERVE

crusty bread

steamed vegetables

NUTRITIONAL INFORMATION

Calories 278

Protein 29g

Carbohydrate 20g

Sugars 10g

Fat 10g

Saturates 5g

variation

Replace the beef with fresh lean ground lamb, if you prefer. Use another type of cheese instead of the Parmesan cheese, if you like.

cook's tip

Store dried herbs in airtight containers or jars in a cool place and away from direct sunlight to retain their aroma and color.

1 Preheat the oven to 375°F/190°C. In a large, heavy-bottom skillet, dry-fry the beef and onion over low heat, stirring frequently, for 4–5 minutes, or until the meat is browned all over. Stir in the dried mixed herbs, flour, beef stock, and tomato paste and season to taste with salt and pepper. Bring to a boil, lower the heat, and let simmer gently for 30 minutes, or until the mixture has thickened.

2 Transfer the mixture to an ovenproof gratin dish. Cover with a layer of the sliced tomatoes, then add a layer of sliced zucchini. Blend the cornstarch with a little milk to make a smooth paste. Pour the remaining milk into a pan and bring to a boil. Add the cornstarch mixture and cook, stirring, for 1–2 minutes, or until thickened. Remove from the heat and beat in the mascarpone cheese and egg yolk. Season to taste with salt and pepper.

3 Spread the white sauce over the layer of zucchinis. Place the dish on a cookie sheet and sprinkle with grated Parmesan cheese. Bake in the preheated oven for 25–30 minutes, or until the topping is golden brown and bubbling. Serve with crusty bread and steamed vegetables.

asparagus & cheese tart

serves 6

prep: 10 mins, plus 30 mins chilling

cook: 50 mins

Fresh asparagus is now readily available all year round, so you can make this tasty supper dish at any time.

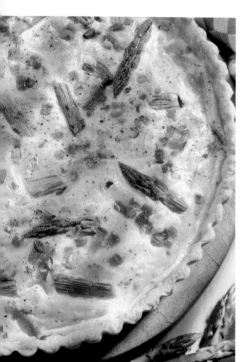

INGREDIENTS

9 oz/250 g ready-made unsweetened
pie dough, thawed if frozen

all-purpose flour, for dusting

9 oz/250 g asparagus

1 tbsp vegetable oil

1 red onion, finely chopped

1 tbsp hazelnuts, chopped

7 oz/200 g goat cheese

2 eggs, beaten

4 tbsp light cream

salt and pepper

NUTRITIONAL INFORMATION

Calories	.360
Protein	.11g
Carbohydrate	.23g
Sugars	.4g
Fat	.25g
Saturates	.10g

variation

Omit the hazelnuts and sprinkle grated Parmesan cheese over the top of the tart just before cooking in the oven, if you prefer.

1 Roll out the pie dough on a lightly floured counter and use to line a 9½-inch/24-cm loose-bottom tart pan. Prick the bottom of the dough with a fork and let chill in the refrigerator for 30 minutes.

2 Preheat the oven to 375°F/190°C. Line the pastry shell with foil and baking beans or pie weights and bake in a preheated oven for 15 minutes. Remove the foil and baking beans and cook for an additional 15 minutes.

3 Cook the asparagus in boiling water for 2–3 minutes, drain and cut into bite-size pieces. Heat the oil in a small skillet and cook the onion over low heat, stirring occasionally, until soft and lightly golden. Spoon the asparagus, onion, and hazelnuts into the prepared pastry shell.

4 Beat the cheese, eggs, and cream together until smooth. Alternatively, process in a blender until smooth. Season well with salt and pepper, then pour the mixture over the asparagus, onion, and hazelnuts. Bake in the preheated oven for 15–20 minutes, or until the cheese filling is just set. Serve warm or cold.

onion tart

cook: 55 mins **prep: 10 mins, plus 30 mins chilling** **serves 4**

This crisp pastry shell is filled with a tasty mixture of onions and cheese and baked until it melts in the mouth.

NUTRITIONAL INFORMATION

Calories	.394
Protein	.11g
Carbohydrate	.29g
Sugars	.7g
Fat	.27g
Saturates	.12g

INGREDIENTS

9 oz/250 g ready-made unsweetened pie dough, thawed if frozen

all-purpose flour, for dusting

3 tbsp butter

2¾ oz/75 g bacon, chopped

1 lb 9 oz/700 g onions, thinly sliced

2 eggs, beaten

generous ⅓ cup freshly grated Parmesan cheese

1 tsp dried sage

salt and pepper

1

2

3

variation

If you prefer, use red onions instead of ordinary ones and replace the dried sage with thyme or oregano.

1 Roll out the pastry on a lightly floured counter and use to line a 9½-inch/24-cm loose-bottom tart pan. Prick the bottom of the pie dough with a fork and let chill in the refrigerator for 30 minutes.

2 Preheat the oven to 350°F/180°C. Heat the butter in a pan, add the chopped bacon and sliced onions and let sweat over low heat for 25 minutes, or until tender. If the onion slices start to brown, add 1 tablespoon of water to the pan.

3 Add the beaten eggs to the onion mixture and stir in the grated cheese and sage, and season to taste with salt and pepper. Spoon the bacon and onion mixture into the prepared pastry shell.

4 Bake in the preheated oven for 20–30 minutes, or until the filling has just set and the pastry is crisp and golden. Let cool slightly in the pan, then serve warm or cold.

small cakes

If the thought of small cakes makes you think of tiered cake racks filled with over-sweet "fancies" covered in pink frosting or rolled in coconut flakes, think again. This collection of irresistible cake recipes will have you rushing into the kitchen to start baking immediately.

Small cakes are very quick and easy to make, as they do not take long to cook and they are made from simple ingredients. If you have not tasted fairy cakes since childhood birthday parties, it is time to rediscover their delights, for fairy cakes have grown up and are now piled up and served at the most sophisticated gatherings. Enjoy the unusual fragrance of Lavender Fairy Cakes (see page 160) or tangy Lemon Butterfly Cakes (see page 162). Many of the easiest cakes in this section, such as Cappuccino Squares (see page 164), Walnut & Cinnamon Blondies (see page 166), or Mincemeat Crumble Bars (see page 168), are baked as tray-bakes in one large pan, then cut into squares to serve. These are also ideal for cake stalls at fêtes and fund-raising events, but you might need to hide them from the family if you don't want them to disappear before you get them packed up. Meringues are always great favorites, and there are recipes here for Brown Sugar Meringues (see page 171) with a lovely caramel flavor and delicate Strawberry Rose Meringues (see page 172). Traditional fare such as Buttermilk Biscuits (see page 184), griddle-cooked Welsh Cakes (see page 186), and Scotch Pancakes (see page 188) are also included, alongside recipes for mouthwatering muffins. Savory Cheese Muffins (see page 193) or Bacon & Cornmeal Muffins (see page 192) are ideal for serving at breakfast or to accompany soups.

lavender fairy cakes

makes 12

prep: 15 mins, plus
20 mins cooling

cook: 12–15 mins

Lavender might seem like an unusual ingredient, but it gives a special fragrance and flavor to these little cakes.

INGREDIENTS

generous ½ cup golden superfine sugar

4 oz/115 g butter, softened

2 eggs, beaten

1 tbsp milk

1 tsp finely chopped lavender flowers

½ tsp vanilla extract

1¼ cups self-rising flour, sifted

scant 1½ cups confectioners' sugar

TO DECORATE

lavender flowers

silver dragées

NUTRITIONAL INFORMATION

Calories 217

Protein 3g

Carbohydrate 33g

Sugars 23g

Fat 9g

Saturates 6g

variation

Add a little purple food coloring to the frosting to give it a pale lilac color to complement the lavender.

cook's tip

Always make sure that your lavender flowers are suitable to eat and free from any chemical sprays or insecticides.

1 Preheat the oven to 400°F/200°C. Place 12 paper cake cases in a muffin pan. Place the superfine sugar and butter in a bowl and cream together until pale and fluffy. Gradually beat in the eggs. Stir in the milk, lavender, and vanilla extract, then carefully fold in the flour.

2 Divide the mixture between the paper cases and bake in the oven for 12–15 minutes, or until well risen and golden. The sponge should bounce back when pressed. A few minutes before the cakes are ready, sift the confectioners' sugar into a bowl and stir in enough water to make a thick frosting.

3 When the cakes are baked, transfer to a wire rack and place a blob of frosting in the center of each one, allowing it to run across the cake. Decorate with lavender flowers and silver dragées and serve as soon as the cakes are cool.

lemon butterfly cakes

makes 12   **prep: 20 mins, plus 30 mins cooling**   **cook: 15–20 mins**

Butterfly cakes may remind you of children's parties, but these attractive, creamy, miniature delights are for adults too!

INGREDIENTS

generous ¾ cup self-rising flour

½ tsp baking powder

4 oz/115 g butter, softened

generous ½ cup golden superfine sugar

2 eggs, beaten

finely grated rind of ½ lemon

2–4 tbsp milk

confectioners' sugar, for dusting

FILLING

¼ cup butter

generous 1 cup confectioners' sugar

1 tbsp lemon juice

NUTRITIONAL INFORMATION

Calories	.227
Protein	.2g
Carbohydrate	.28g
Sugars	.20g
Fat	.13g
Saturates	.8g

variation

To make these cakes extra special, place a few slices of strawberry on top of each one.

cook's tip

If time is limited and you want to speed things up, then the cake batter could be mixed in a food processor, rather than by hand.

1 Preheat the oven to 375°F/190°C. Place 12 paper cases in a muffin pan. Sift the flour and baking powder into a bowl. Add the butter, sugar, eggs, lemon rind, and enough milk to give a medium–soft consistency. Beat thoroughly until smooth. Divide the batter between the paper cases and bake in the preheated oven for 15–20 minutes, or until well risen and golden. Transfer to wire racks to cool.

2 To make the filling, place the butter in a bowl, then sift in the confectioners' sugar and add the lemon juice. Beat well until smooth and creamy. When the cakes are quite cold, use a sharp-pointed vegetable knife to cut a circle from the top of each cake, then cut each circle in half.

3 Spoon a little of the buttercream into the center of each cake and press the 2 semi-circular pieces into it to resemble wings. Dust the cakes with sifted confectioners' sugar before serving.

cappuccino squares

makes 15

prep: 10 mins, plus 30 mins cooling

cook: 35–40 mins

These cakes are made by the all-in-one method and baked in one pan, so they are very easy to put together. They are perfect for the cake stall at fêtes, or to complement a cup of drinking chocolate.

INGREDIENTS

8 oz/225 g butter, softened, plus extra for greasing

generous 1½ cups self-rising flour

1 tsp baking powder

1 tsp unsweetened cocoa, plus extra for dusting

generous 1 cup golden superfine sugar

4 eggs, beaten

3 tbsp instant coffee powder, dissolved in 2 tbsp hot water

WHITE CHOCOLATE FROSTING

4 oz/115 g white chocolate, broken into pieces

2 oz/55 g butter, softened

3 tbsp milk

1¾ cups confectioners' sugar

NUTRITIONAL INFORMATION

Calories 357

Protein 4g

Carbohydrate 44g

Sugars 33g

Fat 20g

Saturates 12g

variation

Use chocolate coffee beans as an extra decoration, placing one chocolate bean on each square.

cook's tip

When melting the frosting ingredients, make sure that the base of the bowl does not touch the simmering water, otherwise the chocolate will seize and become unusable.

1 Preheat the oven to 350°F/180°C. Grease and line the bottom of a shallow 11 x 7-inch/ 28 x 18-cm pan. Sift the flour, baking powder, and cocoa into a bowl and add the butter, superfine sugar, eggs, and coffee. Beat well, by hand or with an electric whisk, until smooth, then spoon into the pan and smooth the top.

2 Bake in the oven for 35–40 minutes, or until risen and firm. Let cool in the pan for 10 minutes, then turn out onto a wire rack and peel off the lining paper. Let cool completely. To make the frosting, place the chocolate, butter, and milk in a bowl set over a pan of simmering water and stir until the chocolate has melted.

3 Remove the bowl from the pan and sift in the confectioners' sugar. Beat until smooth, then spread over the cake. Dust the top of the cake with sifted cocoa, then cut into squares.

walnut & cinnamon blondies

makes 9

prep: 10 mins, plus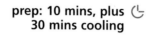
30 mins cooling

cook: 25–30 mins

Blondies are brownies without the chocolate! They taste just as delicious served with a hot cup of coffee.

INGREDIENTS

4 oz/115 g butter, plus extra
for greasing

generous 1 cup brown sugar

1 egg

1 egg yolk

1 cup self-rising flour

1 tsp ground cinnamon

generous ½ cup coarsely
chopped walnuts

NUTRITIONAL INFORMATION

Calories	.325
Protein	.4g
Carbohydrate	.38g
Sugars	.27g
Fat	.18g
Saturates	.8g

1 Preheat the oven to 350°F/180°C. Grease and line the bottom of a 7-inch/18-cm square cake pan. Place the butter and sugar in a pan over low heat and stir until the sugar has dissolved. Cook, stirring, for an additional 1 minute. The mixture will bubble slightly, but do not let it boil. Let cool for 10 minutes.

2 Stir the egg and egg yolk into the mixture. Sift in the flour and cinnamon, add the nuts, and stir until just blended. Pour the cake batter into the prepared pan, then bake in the preheated oven for 20–25 minutes, or until springy in the center and a skewer inserted into the center of the cake comes out clean.

3 Let cool in the pan for a few minutes, then run a knife round the edge of the cake to loosen it. Turn the cake out onto a wire rack and peel off the paper. Let cool completely. When cold, cut into squares.

cook's tip

Do not chop the walnuts too finely, as the blondies should have a good texture and a slight crunch to them.

mocha brownies

🕘 cook: 30–35 mins

🕙 prep: 10 mins, plus 30 mins cooling

makes 16

A hint of coffee gives these brownies a sophisticated flavor. They make an ideal mid-afternoon treat.

NUTRITIONAL INFORMATION

Calories 160

Protein 2g

Carbohydrate 21g

Sugars 16g

Fat 8g

Saturates 4g

INGREDIENTS

2 oz/55 g butter, plus extra for greasing

4 oz/115 g semisweet chocolate, broken into pieces

scant 1 cup brown sugar

2 eggs

1 tbsp instant coffee powder dissolved in 1 tbsp hot water, cooled

scant ⅔ cup all-purpose flour

½ tsp baking powder

⅓ cup coarsely chopped pecans

cook's tip

The brownies will sink slightly and crack as they cool—this is perfectly normal, and gives them their delicious, dense texture.

1 Preheat the oven to 350°F/180°C. Grease and line the bottom of an 8-inch/20-cm square cake pan. Place the chocolate and butter in a heavy-bottom pan over low heat until melted. Stir and let cool.

2 Place the sugar and eggs in a large bowl and cream together until light and fluffy. Fold in the chocolate mixture and cooled coffee and mix thoroughly. Sift in the flour and baking powder and lightly fold into the mixture, then carefully fold in the pecans.

3 Pour the batter into the prepared pan and bake in the preheated oven for 25–30 minutes, or until firm and a skewer inserted into the center comes out clean.

4 Let cool in the pan for a few minutes, then run a knife round the edge of the cake to loosen it. Turn the cake out onto a wire rack and peel off the lining paper. Let cool completely. When cold, cut into squares.

mincemeat crumble bars

makes 12

prep: 20 mins, plus ⏲
1 hr chilling/cooling

cook: 32–35 mins ⏲

These crumble bars make a change from standard, traditional mince pies, but don't just serve them over the festive season; they are bound to be popular at any time of year!

INGREDIENTS

1⅓ cups ready-made mincemeat

confectioners' sugar, for dusting

TOPPING

generous ¾ cup self-rising flour

6 tbsp butter, cut into pieces

scant ½ cup golden superfine sugar

¼ cup slivered almonds

BOTTOM LAYER

5 oz/140 g butter, plus

extra for greasing

scant ½ cup golden superfine sugar

1 cup all-purpose flour

scant ⅔ cup cornstarch

variation

Add a teaspoon of ground cinnamon or ground allspice to the topping mix for a little extra flavor.

cook's tip

Make sure that you bake the bottom layer thoroughly. If it is undercooked, it will not be crisp enough.

1 Grease a shallow 11 x 8-inch/28 x 20-cm cake pan. To make the bottom layer, place the butter and sugar in a bowl and cream together until light and fluffy. Sift in the flour and cornstarch and, with your hands, bring the mixture together to form a ball. Push the dough into the cake pan, pressing it out and into the corners, then chill in

the refrigerator for 20 minutes. Preheat the oven to 400°F/ 200°C. Bake the bottom layer in the oven for 12–15 minutes, or until puffed and golden.

2 To make the crumble topping, place the flour, butter, and sugar in a bowl and rub together into coarse crumbs. Stir in the almonds.

3 Spread the mincemeat over the bottom layer and scatter the crumbs on top. Bake in the oven for an additional 20 minutes, or until golden. Let cool slightly, then cut into 12 pieces and let cool completely. Dust with sifted confectioners' sugar, then serve.

coconut & cherry cakes

makes 8

prep: 15 mins, plus ⏲
20 mins cooling

cook: 20–25 mins ⏲

Coconut makes these little cakes very moist, and gives them a sweet flavor that will make them a hit with children.

INGREDIENTS

4 oz/115 g butter, softened

generous ½ cup golden superfine sugar

2 tbsp milk

2 eggs, beaten

⅔ cup self-rising flour

½ tsp baking powder

1 cup dry unsweetened coconut

generous ½ cup candied cherries, quartered

NUTRITIONAL INFORMATION

Calories	.320
Protein	.4g
Carbohydrate	.34g
Sugars	.26g
Fat	.20g
Saturates	.14g

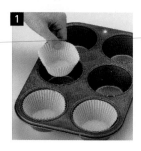

variation

Currants, chopped dried apricots, or dried blueberries could be used instead of cherries.

1 Preheat the oven to 350°F/180°C. Line 1 or 2 muffin pans with 8 paper muffin cases. Place the butter and sugar in a bowl and cream together until light and fluffy, then stir in the milk.

2 Gradually beat in the eggs. Sift in the flour and baking powder and fold in with the coconut. Gently fold in most of the cherries. Spoon the batter into the paper cases and scatter the remaining cherries on top.

3 Bake in the preheated oven for 20–25 minutes, or until well risen, golden, and firm to the touch. Transfer to a wire rack to cool.

brown sugar meringues

cook: 2–3 hrs

prep: 30 mins, plus 20 mins cooling

makes 18

The brown sugar in these meringues creates a wonderful rich caramel flavor while they are baking.

NUTRITIONAL INFORMATION

Calories 102

Protein 1g

Carbohydrate 11g

Sugars 11g

Fat 7g

Saturates 4g

INGREDIENTS

3 egg whites

scant 1 cup brown sugar, strained, plus extra for sprinkling

1¼ cups whipping cream

variation

For hazelnut meringues, sprinkle chopped toasted hazelnuts over the meringues before baking.

1 Preheat the oven to 225°F/110°C. Line 2 large cookie sheets with nonstick parchment paper. Place the egg whites in a large, spotlessly clean, greasefree bowl and whisk until stiff peaks form.

2 Very gradually whisk in the sugar, a spoonful at a time, making sure that you whisk the mixture well between each addition to ensure that the sugar has dissolved and blended with the egg whites. Place spoonfuls of the mixture on the prepared cookie sheets. Sprinkle a little sugar on top of each one.

3 Bake in the preheated oven for 2–3 hours, or until dry, swapping over the position of the cookie sheets halfway through the cooking time. Let cool. Place the cream in a bowl and whip until thick. Join the meringues together in pairs with the cream and serve.

strawberry rose meringues

makes 12

prep: 30 mins, plus ⏲ **20 mins cooling**

cook: 1 hr ⏲

Rose water gives an exotic fragrance to the delicious whipped cream filling in these attractive strawberry meringues.

INGREDIENTS

2 egg whites

generous ½ cup superfine sugar

FILLING

⅓ cup strawberries

2 tsp confectioners' sugar

3 tbsp rose water

⅔ cup heavy cream

TO DECORATE

12 fresh strawberries

rose petals

NUTRITIONAL INFORMATION

Calories 104

Protein 1g

Carbohydrate 12g

Sugars 12g

Fat 6g

Saturates 4g

variation

You can substitute raspberries for the strawberries, or use a mixture of the 2 fruits, if you like.

cook's tip

When sugar is whisked into egg whites to make a meringue, it should gradually dissolve into the egg whites. Make sure the bowl is very clean, otherwise the meringue will not hold its shape.

1 Preheat the oven to 225°F/110°C. Line 2 large cookie sheets with nonstick parchment paper. Place the egg whites in a large, spotlessly clean, greasefree bowl and whisk until stiff peaks form. Whisk in half the sugar, then carefully fold in the remainder.

2 Spoon the meringue into a pastry bag fitted with a large star nozzle. Make 24 x 3-inch/7.5-cm lengths onto the cookie sheets. Bake in the oven for 1 hour, or until the meringues are dry and crisp. Cool on wire racks.

3 To make the filling, place the strawberries in a blender or food processor and process to a purée. Strain the purée into a bowl and stir in the confectioners' sugar and rose water. Place the cream in a separate bowl and whip until thick. Stir into the strawberry mixture and mix well together.

4 Join the meringues together with the strawberry cream. Cut 6 of the strawberries in half and use to decorate the meringues. Scatter rose petals over the top and serve immediately with the remaining whole strawberries.

cherry & golden raisin rockies

makes 10 **prep: 10 mins, plus 30 mins cooling** **cook: 10–15 mins**

Rock cakes are always popular, and are quick and easy to make. To be at their best, they should be eaten the day they are made.

INGREDIENTS

6 tbsp butter, plus extra for greasing

1¾ cups self-rising flour

1 tsp ground allspice

scant ½ cup golden superfine sugar

¼ cup candied cherries, quartered

⅓ cup golden raisins

1 egg

2 tbsp milk

raw brown sugar, for sprinkling

[handwritten annotations: ¼ cup; ⅛ cup; ¾ cup; 1½ TBS p. powder; 2 egg]

NUTRITIONAL INFORMATION

Calories	224
Protein	3g
Carbohydrate	37g
Sugars	18g
Fat	8g
Saturates	5g

variation

Mixed dry fruit could be used as an alternative to the cherries and sultanas in these rock cakes.

1 Preheat the oven to 400°F/200°C, then grease a cookie sheet. Sift the flour and allspice into a bowl. Add the butter and rub it in until the mixture resembles bread crumbs. Stir in the sugar, cherries, and golden raisins.

2 Break the egg into a bowl and whisk in the milk. Pour most of the egg mixture into the dry ingredients and mix with a fork to make a stiff, coarse dough, adding the rest of the egg and milk, if necessary.

3 Using 2 forks, pile the mixture into 10 rocky heaps on the prepared cookie sheet. Sprinkle with raw brown sugar. Bake in the oven for 10–15 minutes, or until golden and firm to the touch. Let cool on the cookie sheet for 2 minutes, then transfer to a wire rack to cool completely.

cook's tip

Rockies are a cross between a cookie and a cake. When you place the uncooked mixture on the cookie sheet, do not worry about making neat piles—they should look rocky, as their name implies!

apple & cinnamon muffins

makes 6　　　　**prep: 15 mins** ⟲　　　　**cook: 20–25 mins** ⏲

These spicy muffins are quick and easy to make with a few stock ingredients and two small apples. The crunchy sugar topping turns them into a truly fruity treat.

INGREDIENTS

⅔ cup whole-wheat all-purpose flour

½ cup white all-purpose flour

1½ tsp baking powder

pinch of salt

1 tsp ground cinnamon

scant ¼ cup golden superfine sugar

2 small eating apples, peeled, cored, and finely chopped

½ cup milk

1 egg, beaten

2 oz/55 g butter, melted

TOPPING

12 brown sugar cubes, coarsely crushed

½ tsp ground cinnamon

NUTRITIONAL INFORMATION

Calories 250

Protein 5g

Carbohydrate 38g

Sugars 20g

Fat 10g

Saturates 6g

variation

If you like, you can split this mixture into 12 portions to make small muffins.

cook's tip

Work quickly once you have chopped the apple, as the flesh soon starts to brown on exposure to the air.

1 Preheat the oven to 400°F/200°C. Line 6 holes of a muffin pan with paper muffin cases.

2 Sift the 2 flours, baking powder, salt, and cinnamon into a large bowl and stir in the sugar and chopped apples. Place the milk, egg, and butter in a separate bowl and mix. Add the wet ingredients to the dry ingredients and gently stir until just combined.

3 Divide the mixture between the paper cases. To make the topping, mix together the crushed sugar cubes and cinnamon and sprinkle over the muffins.

Bake in the preheated oven for 20–25 minutes, or until risen and golden. Serve the muffins warm or cold.

triple chocolate muffins

makes 11 **prep: 15 mins** 🕒 **cook: 20 mins** 🕒

Packed with melting semisweet and white chocolate, these creamy muffins are a chocoholic's delight.

INGREDIENTS

1¾ cups all-purpose flour

¼ cup unsweetened cocoa

2 tsp baking powder

½ tsp baking soda

generous ½ cup semisweet chocolate chips

generous ½ cup white chocolate chips

2 eggs, beaten

1¼ cups sour cream

scant ½ cup brown sugar

6 tbsp butter, melted

NUTRITIONAL INFORMATION

Calories 340

Protein 6g

Carbohydrate 39g

Sugars 20g

Fat 19g

Saturates 11g

1 Preheat the oven to 400°F/200°C. Line 11 holes of 1 or 2 muffin pans with paper muffin cases. Sift the flour, cocoa, baking powder, and baking soda into a large bowl, add the semisweet and white chocolate chips, and stir.

2 Place the eggs, sour cream, sugar, and butter in a separate bowl and mix. Add the wet ingredients to the dry ingredients and stir gently until just combined.

3 Using 2 forks, divide the batter between the paper cases and bake in the preheated oven for 20 minutes, or until well risen and firm to the touch. Serve warm or cold.

cook's tip

As with all muffins, these chocolate delights taste best if they are eaten fresh, on the day they are made.

lemon & ricotta pancakes

⏱ **cook: 20–30 mins**   ⏱ **prep: 10 mins**   **makes 15**

*These thick, soft pancakes can be served for breakfast or lunch,
or as a delicious and unusual dessert.*

NUTRITIONAL INFORMATION

Calories	.88
Protein	.3g
Carbohydrate	.8g
Sugars	.6g
Fat	.5g
Saturates	.3g

INGREDIENTS

scant 1¼ cups ricotta cheese

5 tbsp golden superfine sugar

3 large eggs, separated

finely grated rind of 1 lemon

2 tbsp melted butter

6 tbsp all-purpose flour

warmed cherry or blueberry jelly,

to serve

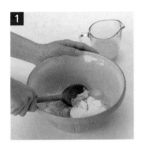  

cook's tip

Do not spread the pancake batter too thinly in the skillet—the finished pancakes should measure about 4–5 inches/ 10–13 cm across.

1 Place the ricotta cheese, sugar, and egg yolks in a large bowl and mix together. Stir in the lemon rind and melted butter. Sift in the flour and fold in. Place the egg whites in a separate, spotlessly clean bowl and whisk until soft peaks form. Gently fold the egg whites into the ricotta mixture.

2 Set a large, nonstick skillet over medium heat and add heaping tablespoonfuls of batter, allowing room for them to spread. Cook for 1–2 minutes, or until the underside is colored, then turn over with a spatula and cook on the other side for an additional 2 minutes.

3 Wrap in a clean dish towel to keep warm until all the pancakes are cooked. Serve with the warmed jelly.

apple shortcakes

cook: 25 mins   **prep: 25 mins**   **makes 4**

NUTRITIONAL INFORMATION

Calories 511

Protein 5g

Carbohydrate 73g

Sugars 44g

Fat 24g

Saturates 15g

variation

Substitute the apples with other fruits, such as pears and replace the ground cinnamon with ground nutmeg.

This American-style dessert is a sweet biscuit, split and filled with sliced apples and whipped cream. The shortcakes can be eaten warm or cold.

INGREDIENTS

2 tbsp butter, cut into small pieces, plus
extra for greasing
generous 1 cup all-purpose flour, plus
extra for dusting
½ tsp salt
1 tsp baking powder
1 tbsp superfine sugar
¼ cup milk
confectioners' sugar, for dusting

FILLING

3 dessert apples, peeled, cored,
and sliced
½ cup superfine sugar
1 tbsp lemon juice
1 tsp ground cinnamon
1¼ cups water
⅔ cup heavy cream,
lightly whipped

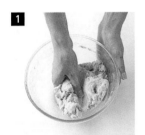

cook's tip

Store the plain shortcakes in an airtight container for 3–5 days. If they are already filled, then store in the refrigerator for 24 hours.

1 Preheat the oven to 425°F/220°C. Lightly grease a cookie sheet. Sift the flour, salt, and baking powder into a large bowl. Stir in the sugar, then add the butter and rub it in with your fingertips until the mixture resembles fine bread crumbs. Pour in the milk and mix to a soft dough.

2 On a lightly floured counter, knead the dough lightly, then roll out to ½-inch/1-cm thick. Stamp out 4 circles, using a 2-inch/5-cm cutter. Transfer the circles to the prepared cookie sheet.

3 Bake in the oven for 15 minutes, until the shortcakes are well risen and lightly browned. Let cool.

4 To make the filling, place the apple, sugar, lemon juice, and cinnamon in a pan. Add the water, bring to a boil and let simmer, uncovered, for 5–10 minutes, or until the apples are tender. Cool slightly, then remove the apples from the pan.

5 To serve, split the shortcakes in half.

Place each bottom half on an individual serving plate and spoon on a quarter of the apple slices, then the cream. Place the other half of the shortcake on top. Serve dusted with confectioners' sugar.

cherry biscuits

makes 8   **prep: 10 mins** ⏲   **cook: 10 mins** ⏲

These are an alternative to traditional biscuits, using sweet candied cherries, which not only create color, but add a distinct flavor.

INGREDIENTS

6 tbsp butter, cut into small pieces, plus
extra for greasing
1½ cups self-rising flour
1–2 tsp superfine sugar
pinch of salt
¼ cup candied cherries, chopped
¼ cup golden raisins
1 egg, beaten
¼ cup milk
all-purpose flour, for dusting

NUTRITIONAL INFORMATION

Calories	.211
Protein	.4g
Carbohydrate	.31g
Sugars	.10g
Fat	.9g
Saturates	.6g

cook's tip

These biscuits will freeze very successfully but they are best thawed and eaten within 1 month. Make sure that they are thoroughly thawed before serving.

1 Preheat the oven to 425°F/220°C. Lightly grease a cookie sheet with a little butter. Sift the flour, sugar, and salt into a large bowl. Add the butter and rub it in with your fingertips until the mixture resembles bread crumbs. Stir in the candied cherries and golden raisins. Add the egg. Set aside 1 tablespoon of the milk for glazing, then add the remainder to the mixture. Mix together to form a soft dough.

2 On a lightly floured counter, roll out the dough to a thickness of ¾ inch/2 cm and cut out 8 biscuits, using a 2-inch/5-cm cutter. Place the biscuits on the cookie sheet and brush the tops with the reserved milk.

3 Bake in the preheated oven for 8–10 minutes, or until the biscuits are golden brown. Let cool on a wire rack, then serve split and buttered, if you like.

molasses biscuits

cook: 10 mins　　　**prep: 10 mins**　　　**serves 8**

These biscuits are light and buttery like traditional biscuits, but they have a deliciously rich flavor which comes from the molasses.

NUTRITIONAL INFORMATION

Calories 208

Protein 4g

Carbohydrate 30g

Sugars 9g

Fat 9g

Saturates 6g

INGREDIENTS

6 tbsp butter, cut into small pieces, plus
extra for greasing

1½ cups self-rising flour

1 tbsp superfine sugar

pinch of salt

1 dessert apple, peeled, cored,
and chopped

1 egg, beaten

2 tbsp molasses

5 tbsp milk

all-purpose flour, for dusting

cook's tip

These biscuits can be frozen, but are best thawed and eaten within 1 month. Before freezing, make sure that they are completely cold.

1 Preheat the oven to 425°F/220°C, then lightly grease a large cookie sheet with a little butter. Sift the flour, sugar, and salt into a large bowl. Add the butter and rub it in with your fingertips until the mixture resembles fine bread crumbs. Stir the apple into the mixture until thoroughly combined.

2 Mix the beaten egg, molasses, and milk together in a measuring cup. Add to the dry ingredients and mix well to form a soft dough.

3 On a lightly floured counter, roll out the dough to a thickness of ¾ inch/2 cm and cut out 8 biscuits, using a 2-inch/5-cm cutter.

4 Arrange the biscuits on the cookie sheet and bake in the preheated oven for 8–10 minutes. Transfer the biscuits to a wire rack and let cool slightly. Serve split in half and spread with butter, if you like.

buttermilk biscuits

makes 8   **prep: 15 mins** ⟳   **cook: 12–15 mins** ⟳

Buttermilk makes these delicious biscuits taste extra light and gives them an especially tangy flavor.

INGREDIENTS

2 oz/55 g cold butter, cut into pieces, plus extra for greasing

generous 2 cups self-rising flour, plus extra for dusting

1 tsp baking powder

pinch of salt

scant ¼ cup golden superfine sugar

1¼ cups buttermilk

2 tbsp milk

TO SERVE

whipped cream

strawberry jelly

NUTRITIONAL INFORMATION

Calories 210

Protein 5g

Carbohydrate 36g

Sugars 8g

Fat 6g

Saturates 4g

variation

These biscuits also taste delicious topped with whipped cream and sliced fresh strawberries.

cook's tip

Dip the cutter in a little flour to prevent it sticking to the dough when you cut out the biscuit circles.

1 Preheat the oven to 425°F/220°C, then grease a cookie sheet. Sift the flour, baking powder, and salt into a bowl. Add the butter and rub in until the mixture resembles fine bread crumbs. Add the sugar and buttermilk and quickly mix together.

2 Turn the mixture out onto a floured counter and knead lightly. Roll out to 1-inch/2.5-cm thick. Using a 2½-inch/6-cm plain or fluted cutter, stamp out biscuits and place on the prepared cookie sheet. Gather the trimmings, re-roll, and stamp out more biscuits until all the dough is used up.

3 Brush the tops of the biscuits with milk. Bake in the preheated oven for 12–15 minutes, or until well risen and golden. Transfer to a wire rack to cool. Split and serve with whipped cream and strawberry jelly.

welsh cakes

makes 16 **prep: 15 mins** ⏲ **cook: 18 mins** ⏲

You do not even have to light the oven to make these little biscuits. They were traditionally cooked on a flat griddle over a fire, but a heavy skillet on top of the stove works just as well!

INGREDIENTS

generous 1½ cups self-rising flour

pinch of salt

2 oz/55 g white cooking fat

2 oz/55 g butter, plus extra for greasing

scant ½ cup golden superfine sugar

generous ½ cup currants

1 egg, beaten

1 tbsp milk (optional)

superfine sugar, for dusting

NUTRITIONAL INFORMATION

Calories	143
Protein	. . . . .2g
Carbohydrate	. . . . .20g
Sugars	. . . . .9g
Fat	. . . . .7g
Saturates	. . . . .3g

variation

You can substitute raisins, golden raisins, or chopped candied cherries for the currants, if you prefer.

cook's tip

Make sure that the heat under the griddle or skillet remains low during cooking to avoid burning the surface of the biscuits.

1 Sift the flour and salt into a bowl. Add the white cooking fat and butter and rub it in until the mixture resembles bread crumbs. Stir in the sugar and currants. Add the egg and a little milk, if necessary, to make a soft, but not sticky, dough.

2 On a floured counter, roll out the dough to ¼ inch/5 mm thick. Stamp into circles with a 2½-inch/6-cm plain or fluted cutter. Gather the trimmings, re-roll, and stamp out more biscuits until all the dough is used up.

3 Grease a griddle or heavy-bottom skillet and set over low heat. Cook the biscuits for 3 minutes on each side, or until golden brown. Dust generously with superfine sugar and serve warm or cold.

scotch pancakes with orange butter

makes 20   **prep: 15–20 mins** (L   **cook: 15–20 mins**

Traditional Scotch pancakes are sometimes known as drop biscuits, but whatever they are called, they will always be a very welcome sight on the tea table.

INGREDIENTS

generous 1½ cups self-rising flour

2 tsp baking powder

pinch of salt

2 tbsp golden superfine sugar

1 egg

scant 1 cup milk

butter, for greasing

ORANGE BUTTER

6 oz/175 g butter

¼ cup confectioners' sugar, sifted

finely grated rind of 1 orange and

2 tbsp orange juice

variation

As an alternative to the orange butter, serve butter and jelly or honey with the pancakes.

cook's tip

Heat up the griddle or skillet gently and check it is ready by dropping a small amount of pancake batter onto the surface, which should sizzle.

1 To make the orange butter, place all of the ingredients in a bowl and beat together until light and fluffy. Chill in the refrigerator while making the pancakes.

2 To make the pancakes, sift the flour, baking powder, and salt into a bowl. Stir in the sugar and make a well in the center. Place the egg and milk in a separate bowl, whisk together, and pour into the well. Gradually draw the flour into the liquid by stirring with a wooden spoon, then beat thoroughly to make a smooth batter.

3 Grease a griddle or heavy-bottom skillet and set over medium–high heat. Drop spoonfuls of the batter into the pan and cook for 2–3 minutes, or until bubbles burst on the surface and the underside is golden. Turn over with a spatula and cook for an additional 1 minute, or until golden on the other side. Keep warm in a clean dish towel until all the pancakes are cooked. Serve with the orange butter.

fruity muffins

cook: 30 mins | **prep: 10 mins** | **makes 10**

NUTRITIONAL INFORMATION

Calories 162

Protein 4g

Carbohydrate 28g

Sugars 11g

Fat 4g

Saturates 1g

variation

If you like dried figs, they make a deliciously crunchy alternative to the apricots; they also go very well with the flavor of the orange.

Perfect for those on a lowfat diet and for weight watchers, these little cakes contain no butter, just a little corn oil.

INGREDIENTS

1½ cups whole-wheat self-rising flour	1 tsp finely grated orange rind
2 tsp baking powder	1¼ cups skim milk
generous ⅛ cup brown sugar	1 egg, beaten
generous ½ cup no-soak dried apricots, finely chopped	3 tbsp corn oil
	2 tbsp rolled oats
1 medium banana, mashed with 1 tbsp orange juice	fruit spread, honey, or maple syrup, to serve

cook's tip

Corn oil does not have any particular flavor, so is ideal for muffins and cakes. It is sold in most large supermarkets, but if unavailable, then use another lightly flavored oil instead, such as sunflower-seed oil.

1 Preheat the oven to 400°F/200°C. Place 10 paper muffin cases in a deep muffin pan. Sift the flour and baking powder into a large bowl, adding any bran that remains in the strainer. Stir in the sugar and apricots.

2 Make a well in the center of the dry ingredients and add the mashed banana, grated orange rind, milk, beaten egg, and corn oil. Mix together well to form a thick batter.

3 Divide the batter evenly between the 10 paper cases. Sprinkle the tops with a few rolled oats and bake in the preheated oven for 25–30 minutes, or until well risen and firm to the touch or until a skewer inserted into the center comes out clean. Transfer the muffins to a wire rack to cool slightly. Serve the muffins while they are warm with a little fruit spread, honey, or maple syrup.

bacon & cornmeal muffins

makes 12   **prep: 20 mins** ⌛   **cook: 20–25 mins** ⏱

These muffins are delicious served warm for breakfast or as an accompaniment to chicken or game casseroles.

INGREDIENTS

5½ oz/150 g pancetta

generous 1 cup self-rising flour

1 tbsp baking powder

1 tsp salt

1⅔ cups fine cornmeal

¼ cup golden granulated sugar

4 oz/115 g butter, melted

2 eggs, beaten

1¼ cups milk

NUTRITIONAL INFORMATION

Calories 280

Protein 7g

Carbohydrate 31g

Sugars 6g

Fat 15g

Saturates 7g

cook's tip

Pancetta is thin Italian bacon. If it is unavailable, you can use thinly sliced strips of lean bacon instead.

1 Preheat the oven to 400°F/200°C and preheat the broiler to medium. Line 12 holes of 1 or 2 muffin pans with paper muffin cases. Cook the pancetta under the preheated broiler until crisp, then crumble into pieces and set aside until required.

2 Sift the flour, baking powder, and salt into a bowl, then stir in the cornmeal and sugar. Place the butter, eggs, and milk in a separate bowl. Add the wet ingredients to the dry ingredients and mix until just blended.

3 Fold in the pancetta, then divide the mixture between the paper cases and bake in the preheated oven for 20–25 minutes, or until risen and golden. Serve the muffins warm or cold.

cheese muffins

cook: 20–25 mins　　　**prep: 15 mins**　　　　**makes 10**

*These savory muffins are delicious served with soup,
turning it into a filling main meal.*

NUTRITIONAL INFORMATION	
Calories	.260
Protein	.9g
Carbohydrate	.27g
Sugars	.2g
Fat	.13g
Saturates	.7g

INGREDIENTS

generous ¾ cup self-rising flour

1 tbsp baking powder

1 tsp salt

1½ cups fine cornmeal

1½ cups grated mature
Cheddar cheese

2 oz/55 g butter, melted

2 eggs, beaten

1 garlic clove, crushed

1¼ cups milk

cook's tip

Cornmeal, or polenta, used to
be difficult to find, but it is
now widely available in most
major food stores and health
food stores.

1 Preheat the oven
to 400°F/200°C. Line
10 holes of 1 or 2 muffin pans
with paper muffin cases. Sift
the flour, baking powder, and
salt into a bowl, then stir in
the cornmeal and a generous
1 cup of the cheese.

2 Place the melted butter,
eggs, crushed garlic,
and milk in a separate bowl.
Add the wet ingredients to the
dry ingredients and mix gently
until just combined.

3 Using a spoon, divide
the mixture between
the paper cases, scatter over
the remaining cheese, and
bake in the preheated oven for
20–25 minutes, or until risen
and golden brown. Serve
warm or cold.

cheese & chive biscuits

makes 8 **prep: 15 mins** **cook: 10 mins**

Savory biscuits make a delicious alternative to sandwiches when you want a light meal, and they are ideal for serving with soup.

INGREDIENTS

3 tbsp butter, plus extra for greasing

generous ¾ cup white self-rising flour, plus extra for dusting

generous ¾ cup whole-wheat self-rising flour

1 tsp baking powder

pinch of salt

generous ¾ cup finely grated Cheddar cheese

2 tbsp snipped fresh chives

3 tbsp milk

fresh chives, to garnish

NUTRITIONAL INFORMATION

Calories	182
Protein	6g
Carbohydrate	21g
Sugars	1g
Fat	9g
Saturates	5g

cook's tip

Choose a mature, well-flavored Cheddar cheese for these biscuits, to give them a strong, well-rounded taste.

1 Preheat the oven to 425°F/220°C, then grease a cookie sheet. Sift the 2 flours, baking powder, and salt into a bowl. Rub in the butter until the mixture resembles fine bread crumbs, then stir in the grated cheese and chives. Stir in up to 1 tablespoon of milk to make a fairly soft, light dough.

2 On a floured counter, roll out the dough to ¾-inch/2-cm thick and stamp into circles with a 2½-inch/6-cm plain cutter. Gather the trimmings, re-roll, and stamp out more biscuits until the dough is used up.

3 Place the biscuits on the prepared cookie sheet, brush the tops with the remaining milk, and sprinkle with the grated cheese. Bake in the preheated oven for 10 minutes, or until well risen and golden. Garnish with fresh chives and serve warm or cold.

blinis

cook: 20 mins

prep: 20 mins, plus 1 hr standing

makes 8

Blinis are Russian yeast pancakes traditionally made with buckwheat flour, which gives them a tasty and unusual flavor.

NUTRITIONAL INFORMATION

Calories	170
Protein	6g
Carbohydrate	25g
Sugars	3g
Fat	6g
Saturates	2g

INGREDIENTS

generous ¾ cup buckwheat flour

generous ¾ cup strong white bread flour

⅛-oz/7-g envelope active dry yeast

1 tsp salt

1⅓ cups tepid milk

2 eggs, 1 whole and 1 separated

vegetable oil, for brushing

TO SERVE

sour cream

smoked salmon

1 Sift both flours into a large, warmed bowl. Stir in the yeast and salt. Beat in the milk, whole egg, and egg yolk until smooth. Cover the bowl and let stand in a warm place for 1 hour.

2 Place the egg white in a spotlessly clean bowl and whisk until soft peaks form. Fold into the batter. Brush a heavy-bottom skillet with vegetable oil and set over medium–high heat. When the skillet is hot, pour enough of the batter onto the surface to make a blini 4–5 inches/ 10–13 cm across.

3 When bubbles rise, turn the blini over with a spatula and cook the other side until light brown. Wrap in a clean dish towel to keep warm while cooking the remainder. Serve the warm blinis with sour cream and smoked salmon.

variation

If buckwheat flour is unavailable, you can substitute whole-wheat bread flour instead.

large cakes

You only have to look at the crowds round the cake stall at any fund-raising event to know that everyone loves a homemade cake. But no magic is required to produce a wonderful cake that will make a stunning centerpiece at any tea table. The cakes in this section are not complicated, and none of them have elaborate decoration. There are plenty of books dedicated to the art of cake decorating, so the cakes here have simple frostings, colorful fruit toppings, or sticky syrup drizzled over them.

You will find a variety of cakes, from family favorites, such as Cherry & Almond Cake (see page 200) and Carrot Cake (see page 212), to wickedly rich Mississippi Mud Cake (see page 215). There are spicy cakes, such as Preserved Ginger Cake (see page 198) and Honey Spice Cake (see page 207), which fill the kitchen with a fragrant aroma, and moist dessert cakes with fruit. Who could resist Blueberry & Lemon Drizzle Cake (see page 210), Passion Fruit Angel Cake (see page 218), or Pear & Cinnamon Cake (see page 206)? Classic recipes have not been forgotten, and a rich, fruity Christmas Cake has been included (see page 208) along with an easy Victoria Sponge (see page 219), mixed using the all-in-one method. The beauty of this recipe is that you can make endless variations on it once you have mastered the basics.

Some of the cakes are best when freshly made, and others, such as Cherry & Almond Cake, will keep for a few days. Preserved Ginger Cake benefits from being kept for a day or two before serving, though you will probably have trouble resisting it for more than a few hours!

preserved ginger cake

serves 12 **prep: 20 mins, plus 1 hr cooling** **cook: 45–50 mins**

Ground ginger, preserved ginger, and ginger syrup make this a really gingery cake! Its rich flavor is warming and moreish.

INGREDIENTS

4 oz/115 g butter, plus extra
for greasing
generous 1½ cups self-rising flour
1 tbsp ground ginger
1 tsp ground cinnamon
½ tsp baking soda
generous ½ cup brown sugar
grated rind of ½ lemon
2 eggs
1½ tbsp corn syrup
1½ tbsp milk

TOPPING
6 pieces of preserved ginger, plus
4 tbsp ginger syrup from the jar
generous 1 cup confectioners' sugar
lemon juice

NUTRITIONAL INFORMATION

Calories 243

Protein 3g

Carbohydrate 40g

Sugars 25g

Fat 9g

Saturates 6g

variation

If you don't want to decorate the cake with preserved ginger pieces, try a layer of frosting lightly sprinkled with ground cinnamon instead.

 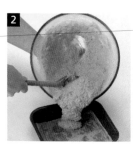 

cook's tip

This cake will taste much better if it is kept in an airtight container for a day before eating, to give the ginger flavor time to develop.

1 Preheat the oven to 325°F/160°C. Grease and line the bottom of a 7-inch/18-cm square cake pan. Sift the flour, ginger, cinnamon, and baking soda into a bowl. Rub in the butter, then stir in the sugar and lemon rind. Make a well in the center. Place the eggs, syrup, and milk in a separate bowl and whisk together. Pour into the dry ingredients and beat until smooth.

2 Pour the batter into the prepared pan and bake in the preheated oven for 45–50 minutes, or until well risen and firm to the touch. Let cool in the pan for 30 minutes, then turn out onto a wire rack and peel off the lining paper. Let cool completely.

3 To make the topping, cut each piece of preserved ginger into quarters and arrange the pieces on top of the cake. Sift the confectioners' sugar into a bowl and stir in the ginger syrup and enough lemon juice to make a smooth frosting. Place the frosting in a plastic bag and cut a tiny hole in one corner. Drizzle the frosting over the cake. Let set, then cut the cake into squares and serve.

cherry & almond cake

serves 8

prep: 15 mins, plus 30 mins cooling

cook: 1 hr 30 mins– 1 hr 45 mins

Ground almonds add richness to this cake and help its keeping qualities. It's sure to become a family favorite.

INGREDIENTS

6 oz/175 g butter, softened, plus extra for greasing

generous 1 cup candied cherries

scant 1 cup golden superfine sugar

3 eggs

⅔ cup ground almonds

generous 1½ cups all-purpose flour

1½ tsp baking powder

generous ⅓ cup slivered almonds

NUTRITIONAL INFORMATION

Calories	518
Protein	8g
Carbohydrate	65g
Sugars	43g
Fat	27g
Saturates	13g

variation

You can substitute chopped no-soak apricots for the candied cherries in this cake, if you prefer.

cook's tip

Washing and drying the candied cherries before using them in the recipe helps prevent them sinking to the bottom of the cake.

1 Preheat the oven to 325°F/160°C. Grease and line the bottom of a deep 7-inch/18-cm cake pan. Cut the cherries in half, then place them in a strainer and rinse to remove all the syrup. Pat dry with paper towels and set aside.

2 Place the butter, superfine sugar, eggs, and ground almonds in a bowl. Sift in the flour and baking powder. Beat thoroughly until smooth, then stir in the cherries. Spoon the batter into the prepared pan and smooth the top.

3 Sprinkle the slivered almonds over the cake. Bake in the preheated oven for 1½–1¾ hours, or until well risen and a skewer inserted into the center of the cake comes out clean. Let cool in the pan for 10 minutes, then turn out onto a wire rack, remove the lining paper, and let cool completely.

caribbean coconut cake

serves 8

prep: 20 mins, plus 30 mins cooling

cook: 25 mins

Dry unsweetened coconut and coconut cream make this moist cake rich and delicious, and are complemented by pineapple jelly.

INGREDIENTS

10 oz/280 g butter, softened, plus extra for greasing

scant 1 cup golden superfine sugar

3 eggs

1¼ cups self-rising flour

1½ tsp baking powder

½ tsp freshly grated nutmeg

⅔ cup dry unsweetened coconut

5 tbsp coconut cream

2¾ cups confectioners' sugar

5 tbsp pineapple jelly

dry unsweetened coconut, toasted, to decorate

NUTRITIONAL INFORMATION

Calories	.694
Protein	.6g
Carbohydrate	.84g
Sugars	.68g
Fat	.40g
Saturates	.27g

cook's tip

Coconut cream comes in small cartons. What remains after making this cake can be used in custards, soups, or curries, or can be poured over fresh fruit in place of cream.

1 Preheat the oven to 350°F/180°C. Grease and line the bottoms of 2 x 8-inch/20-cm sponge cake pans. Place 6 oz/175 g of the butter in a bowl with the sugar and eggs and sift in the flour, baking powder, and nutmeg. Beat together until smooth, then stir in the coconut and 2 tablespoons of the coconut cream.

2 Divide the mixture between the prepared pans and smooth the tops. Bake in the preheated oven for 25 minutes, or until golden and firm to the touch. Let cool in the pans for 5 minutes, then turn out onto a wire rack, peel off the lining paper, and let cool completely.

3 Sift the confectioners' sugar into a bowl and add the remaining butter and coconut cream. Beat together until smooth. Spread the pineapple jelly on one of the cakes and top with just under half of the buttercream. Place the other cake on top. Spread the remaining buttercream on top of the cake and scatter with the toasted coconut.

jewel-topped madeira cake

⏱ **cook: 1 hr 15 mins–
1 hr 30 mins**

⏲ **prep: 25 mins, plus
30 mins cooling**

serves 8

*Brightly colored crystallized fruits make a stunning and unusual
topping for this classic Madeira cake.*

NUTRITIONAL INFORMATION	
Calories	.570
Protein	.7g
Carbohydrate	.81g
Sugars	.55g
Fat	.27g
Saturates	.16g

INGREDIENTS

8 oz/225 g butter, softened, plus
extra for greasing

generous 1 cup golden superfine sugar

finely grated rind of 1 lemon

4 eggs, beaten

2 cups self-rising flour, sifted

2–3 tbsp milk

FRUIT TOPPING

2½ tbsp honey

8 oz/225 g crystallized fruit

variation

Traditionally, a Madeira
cake is simply decorated
with a slice of candied peel
on top, which is placed on
the cake after it has been
cooking for 1 hour.

1 Preheat the oven
to 325°F/160°C. Grease
and line the bottom of a deep
8-inch/20-cm springform cake
pan. Place the butter, sugar,
and lemon rind in a bowl
and beat together until light
and fluffy. Gradually beat
in the eggs. Gently fold in
the flour, alternating with
enough milk to give a soft,
dropping consistency.

2 Spoon the batter
into the prepared pan
and bake in the preheated
oven for 1¼–1½ hours, or until
risen and golden and a skewer
inserted into the center comes
out clean.

3 Let cool in the pan for
10 minutes, then turn
out onto a wire rack and
remove the lining paper. Let
cool completely. To make the
topping, brush the honey over
the cake and arrange the fruit
on top.

banana & lime cake

cook: 45 mins

prep: 35 mins, plus 45 mins cooling

serves 10

This is a substantial cake that is ideal served for tea. The mashed bananas help to keep the cake moist and the lime frosting gives it extra zing and zest.

variation

For a delicious alternative, replace the lime rind and juice with orange and the golden raisins with chopped apricots.

INGREDIENTS

butter, for greasing

scant 2 cups all-purpose flour

1 tsp salt

1½ tsp baking powder

scant ⅞ cup firmly packed brown sugar

1 tsp grated lime rind

1 egg, beaten

1 banana, mashed with 1 tbsp lime juice

⅔ cup lowfat mascarpone cheese

⅔ cup golden raisins

TOPPING

1 cup confectioners' sugar

1–2 tsp lime juice

½ tsp finely grated lime rind

TO DECORATE

banana chips

finely grated lime rind

cook's tip

For optimum flavor, it is best to use an overripe banana in this recipe. Banana chips are available from most large supermarkets and health food stores.

1 Preheat the oven to 350°F/180°C. Grease and line a deep 7-inch/18-cm round cake pan with parchment paper. Sift the flour, salt, and baking powder into a large bowl and stir in the sugar and lime rind.

2 Make a well in the center of the dry ingredients and add the egg, banana, mascarpone cheese, and golden raisins. Mix well until thoroughly incorporated. Spoon the batter into the pan and smooth the surface.

3 Bake in the preheated oven for 40–45 minutes, or until firm to the touch or until a skewer inserted in the center comes out clean. Let the cake cool in the pan for 10 minutes, then turn out onto a wire rack to cool completely.

4 To make the topping, sift the confectioners' sugar into a small bowl and mix with the lime juice to form a soft, but not too runny frosting. Stir in the grated lime rind. Drizzle the frosting over the cake, letting it run down the sides. Decorate the cake with banana chips and lime rind. Let the cake stand for 15 minutes so that the frosting sets.

pear & cinnamon cake

serves 8

prep: 20 mins, plus 30 mins cooling

cook: 55–60 mins

This cake smells wonderful while it is baking, and is a delicious way to end a memorable meal.

INGREDIENTS

3–4 firm pears, depending on the size

1 vanilla bean

8 oz/225 g butter, melted and cooled, plus extra for greasing

scant 1⅓ cups golden superfine sugar

2 large eggs

1¾ cups all-purpose flour

1 tbsp ground cinnamon

½ tsp baking soda

4 tbsp golden confectioners' sugar

NUTRITIONAL INFORMATION

Calories	.508
Protein	.5g
Carbohydrate	.76g
Sugars	.52g
Fat	.23g
Saturates	.14g

variation

As an alternative to fresh pears, canned pears will work almost as well.

1 Peel the pears, cut into quarters, and remove the cores. Cut the pears into small cubes, place in a pan and cover with water. Split the vanilla bean to expose the seeds, and add to the pan. Bring to a boil, then reduce the heat and simmer gently until the pears are tender. Remove from the heat and let cool. Preheat the oven to 350°F/180°C. Thoroughly grease and line the bottom of an 8-inch/20-cm springform cake pan. Drain the pears, reserving their cooking liquid, and pat dry with paper towels.

2 Place the sugar, eggs, and butter in a bowl and whisk together. Sift the flour, cinnamon, and baking soda into a separate bowl. Fold the flour mixture into the sugar and egg mixture, one-third at a time. Fold in the pears.

3 Transfer the batter to the prepared pan and bake in the preheated oven for 50–55 minutes, or until a skewer inserted into the center comes out clean. Let cool in the pan for 20 minutes, then turn out onto a wire rack, peel off the lining paper, and let cool completely.

4 Sift the confectioners' sugar into a bowl and add enough of the reserved pear cooking liquid to give a pouring consistency. Drizzle the frosting over the cake and let set before serving.

honey spice cake

cook: 45–55 mins | **prep: 15 mins, plus 30 mins cooling** | serves 8

This cake can be made in advance, as it benefits from being kept for a day before eating to let the flavors develop.

NUTRITIONAL INFORMATION

Calories 534

Protein 4g

Carbohydrate 97g

Sugars 78g

Fat 17g

Saturates 11g

INGREDIENTS

5½ oz/150 g butter, plus extra
for greasing

generous ½ cup brown sugar

½ cup honey

1 tbsp water

scant 1½ cups self-rising flour

½ tsp ground ginger

½ tsp ground cinnamon

½ tsp caraway seeds

seeds from 8 cardamom pods, ground

2 eggs, beaten

3½ cups confectioners' sugar

cook's tip

Try to choose a strongly flavored honey so that its richness is not totally overpowered by the flavors of all the spices.

1 Preheat the oven to 350°F/180°C. Grease a 3½-cup fluted cake pan. Place the butter, sugar, honey, and water into a heavy-bottom] pan. Set over low heat and stir until the butter has melted and the sugar has dissolved. Remove from the heat and let cool for 10 minutes.

2 Sift the flour into a bowl and mix in the ginger, cinnamon, caraway seeds, and cardamom. Make a well in the center. Pour in the honey mixture and the eggs and beat well until smooth. Pour the batter into the prepared pan and bake in the preheated oven for 40–50 minutes, or until well risen and a skewer inserted into the center comes out clean. Let cool in the pan for 5 minutes, then transfer to a wire rack to cool completely.

3 Sift the confectioners' sugar into a bowl. Stir in enough warm water to make a smooth, flowing frosting. Spoon over the cake, allowing it to flow down the sides, then let set.

christmas cake

serves 24 **prep: 15 mins, plus** ☾ **20 mins cooling** **cook: 3 hrs 10 mins– 3 hrs 40 mins**

This is an easy way of making a Christmas cake, as no creaming or careful folding-in is required. Boiling the fruit mixture first makes the cake taste especially moist and flavorsome.

INGREDIENTS

8 oz/225 g butter, cut into pieces, plus extra for greasing

1½ cups brown sugar

2 tbsp molasses

3 lb 5 oz/1.5 kg luxury dried fruit

finely grated rind and juice of 1 large orange

⅓ cup cognac

5 eggs, beaten

generous 1 cup coarsely chopped mixed nuts

⅔ cup ground almonds

scant 2¼ cups all-purpose flour

½ tsp baking powder

1 tbsp ground allspice

NUTRITIONAL INFORMATION

Calories 330

Protein 5g

Carbohydrate 52g

Sugars 44g

Fat 12g

Saturates 5g

---

variation

You could substitute rum for the cognac, if you would prefer a slightly different taste to this rich fruit cake.

cook's tip

Cover the cake with marzipan and frosting. Alternatively, you can simply top the cake with an arrangement of luxury nuts and dried fruit.

1 Place the butter, sugar, molasses, dried fruit, orange rind and juice, and cognac in a large pan. Bring slowly to a boil, then reduce the heat and simmer gently for 10 minutes, stirring occasionally. Remove from the heat and let cool.

2 Preheat the oven to 300°F/150°C. Grease and line the bottom of a deep 8-inch/20-cm round cake pan and wrap a double layer of paper round the outside of the pan. Stir the eggs, mixed nuts, and ground almonds into the cooled fruit mixture and mix well. Sift in the flour, baking powder, and allspice. Stir in gently but thoroughly. Spoon into the prepared pan and smooth the top.

3 Bake in the oven for 1 hour, then reduce the heat to 275°F/140°C and bake for 2–2½ hours, or until a skewer inserted into the center comes out clean. Let cool in the pan, then turn out and store, wrapped in waxed paper and foil, until ready to decorate.

blueberry & lemon drizzle cake

serves 12 **prep: 20 mins, plus 30 mins cooling** **cook: 1 hr**

The lemon syrup that is poured over this cake gives it a wonderful fresh, tangy flavor—a perfect complement to the blueberries.

INGREDIENTS

8 oz/225 g butter, softened,
plus extra for greasing
generous 1 cup golden superfine sugar
4 eggs, beaten
1¾ cups self-rising flour, sifted
finely grated rind and juice of 1 lemon
generous ¼ cup ground almonds
7 oz/200 g fresh blueberries

TOPPING

juice of 2 lemons
generous ½ cup golden superfine sugar

NUTRITIONAL INFORMATION	
Calories	.364
Protein	.5g
Carbohydrate	.47g
Sugars	.31g
Fat	.19g
Saturates	.11g

cook's tip

If you warm a lemon gently in the microwave for a few seconds on High, it will yield more juice when you squeeze it.

1 Preheat the oven to 350°F/180°C, then grease and line the bottom of an 8-inch/20-cm square cake pan. Place the butter and sugar in a bowl and beat together until light and fluffy. Gradually beat in the eggs, adding a little flour toward the end to prevent curdling. Beat in the lemon rind, then fold in the remaining flour and almonds with enough of the lemon juice to give a good dropping consistency.

2 Fold in three-quarters of the blueberries and turn into the prepared pan. Smooth the surface, then scatter the remaining blueberries on top. Bake in the preheated oven for 1 hour, or until firm to the touch and a skewer inserted into the center comes out clean.

3 To make the topping, place the lemon juice and sugar in a bowl and mix together. As soon as the cake comes out of the oven, prick it all over with a fine skewer and pour over the lemon mixture. Let cool in the pan until completely cold, then cut into 12 squares to serve.

sticky date cake

 cook: 1 hr 10 mins–
1 hr 25 mins

prep: 20 mins, plus
30 mins cooling

serves 8

The toffee topping on this cake makes it very moreish. It can be a comforting or sophisticated dessert, depending on its presentation.

NUTRITIONAL INFORMATION

Calories 534

Protein 6g

Carbohydrate 75g

Sugars 54g

Fat 25g

Saturates 16g

INGREDIENTS

scant 1⅓ cups pitted dates, chopped

1¼ cups boiling water

4 oz/115 g butter, softened, plus extra for greasing

scant 1 cup golden superfine sugar

3 eggs, beaten

generous 1½ cups self-rising flour, sifted

½ tsp ground cinnamon

1 tsp baking soda

TOPPING

scant ½ cup brown sugar

2 oz/55 g butter

3 tbsp heavy cream

cook's tip

Soaking dates for a few minutes in boiling water restores their moisture and gives them a delicious toffee-like consistency ideal for cakes and desserts.

1 Place the dates in a bowl and cover them with the boiling water. Preheat the oven to 350°F/180°C, then grease a 9-inch/23-cm springform cake pan. Place the butter and sugar in a bowl and beat until light and fluffy. Gradually beat in the eggs, then fold in the flour and cinnamon.

2 Add the baking soda to the dates and water, then pour onto the creamed mixture. Stir until well mixed. Pour into the prepared pan and bake in the oven for 1–1¼ hours, or until well risen and firm to the touch.

3 Preheat the broiler to medium. To make the topping, place the sugar, butter, and cream in a pan. Set over low heat, stirring, until the sugar has melted, then bring to a boil and let simmer for 3 minutes. Pour over the cake and place the cake under the preheated broiler until the topping is bubbling. Let cool in the pan until the topping has set, then transfer to a wire rack to cool completely before serving.

carrot cake

serves 8   **prep: 15 mins, plus** 🕐
20 mins cooling/standing

cook: 1 hr 5 mins 🍳

*Carrots give this cake a surprisingly sweet, wholesome
flavor and an attractive golden color.*

INGREDIENTS

butter, for greasing

scant 1 cup brown sugar

3 eggs

¾ cup sunflower or corn oil

1 cup coarsely grated carrots

2 ripe bananas, mashed

⅓ cup chopped walnuts

2 cups all-purpose flour

½ tsp salt

1 tsp baking soda

2 tsp baking powder

FROSTING

scant 1 cup cream cheese

½ tsp vanilla extract

generous 1 cup confectioners' sugar

2 tbsp chopped walnuts

NUTRITIONAL INFORMATION

Calories 650

Protein 9g

Carbohydrate 73g

Sugars 46g

Fat 38g

Saturates 11g

variation

If you prefer, you can bake the
batter in a rectangular pan and cut
the finished cake into squares.

cook's tip

The more coarsely you
grate the carrots, the more
texture this cake will have.
If you prefer a smoother
texture, grate the carrots
a little more finely.

1 Preheat the oven
to 350°F/180°C. Grease
and line the bottom of a
9-inch/23-cm springform cake
pan. Place the sugar, eggs,
sunflower oil, carrots, bananas,
and walnuts in a bowl. Sift in
the flour, salt, baking soda,
and baking powder. Beat the
batter until smooth.

2 Turn the batter into
the prepared pan and
bake in the preheated oven for
1 hour 5 minutes, or until well
risen and golden brown and a
skewer inserted into the center
comes out clean. Let cool in
the pan for 10 minutes, then
turn out and peel off the lining
paper. Transfer to a wire rack
to cool completely.

3 To make the frosting,
place the cream cheese
and vanilla extract in a bowl
and beat well to soften. Beat
in the confectioners' sugar
a tablespoon at a time, until
smooth. Swirl over the cake
and sprinkle the chopped
walnuts on top. Let stand in
a cool place for the frosting to
harden slightly before serving.

coffee caramel cake

serves 8

**prep: 20 mins, plus
20 mins cooling**

cook: 35 mins

*This intensely flavored coffee cake is complemented perfectly
by a soft and deliciously sweet caramel icing.*

INGREDIENTS

6 oz/175 g butter, softened,
plus extra for greasing

scant 1 cup golden superfine sugar

3 eggs, beaten

generous 1½ cups self-rising
flour, sifted

scant ½ cup strong black coffee

chocolate-covered coffee beans,
to decorate

FROSTING

½ cup milk

4½ oz/125 g butter

3 tbsp golden superfine sugar

5¾ cups confectioners' sugar

NUTRITIONAL INFORMATION

Calories	.518
Protein	.6g
Carbohydrate	.51g
Sugars	.30g
Fat	.34g
Saturates	.21g

cook's tip

Take extra care when adding
the warm milk mixture to the
caramel in Step 2, because
the hot liquid may splutter
and burn.

1 Preheat the oven
to 350°F/180°C, then
grease and line the bottom of
2 x 8-inch/20-cm sponge cake
pans. Place the butter and
sugar in a bowl and beat
together until light and fluffy.
Gradually beat in the eggs,
then fold in the flour and
coffee. Divide the batter
between the prepared pans
and bake in the preheated

oven for 30 minutes, or until
well risen and springy when
pressed in the center. Let cool
in the pans for 5 minutes, then
turn out and peel off the lining
paper. Transfer to wire racks
to cool completely.

2 To make the frosting,
place the milk and
butter in a pan, set over low
heat, and stir until the butter

has melted. Remove the pan
from the heat and set aside.
Place the superfine sugar in
a separate, heavy-bottom pan
and set over low heat, stirring
constantly, until the sugar
dissolves and turns a golden
caramel. Remove from the
heat and stir in the warm
milk mixture. Return to the
heat and stir until the
caramel dissolves.

3 Remove from the heat
and gradually stir in the
confectioners' sugar, beating
until the frosting is a smooth
spreading consistency. Join the
cakes together with some of
the frosting and spread the
rest over the top and sides.
Decorate with chocolate-
covered coffee beans.

mississippi mud cake

⏲ **cook: 1 hr 30 mins**   ⏱ **prep: 25 mins, plus 30 mins cooling**   **serves 16**

Mud cake is a rich, dense chocolate cake that can be served with mascarpone or fresh berries, or plain with after-dinner coffee.

NUTRITIONAL INFORMATION

Calories	.344
Protein	.3g
Carbohydrate	.46g
Sugars	.34g
Fat	.17g
Saturates	.11g

INGREDIENTS

8 oz/225 g butter, cut into pieces, plus extra for greasing

5½ oz/150 g semisweet chocolate

generous 2 cups golden superfine sugar

1 cup hot water

3 tbsp Tia Maria or cognac

1¾ cups all-purpose flour

1 tsp baking powder

¼ cup unsweetened cocoa

2 eggs, beaten

TO DECORATE

fresh raspberries

chocolate curls

cook's tip

If the cake starts to brown too quickly while baking, cover the top loosely with a piece of foil for the remainder of the cooking time.

1 Preheat the oven to 325°F/160°C, then grease and line an 8-inch/20-cm round cake pan. Break the chocolate into pieces, then place the butter, chocolate, sugar, hot water, and Tia Maria in a large, heavy-bottom pan over low heat and stir until the chocolate melts.

2 Stir until smooth, transfer the mixture to a large bowl, and let cool for 15 minutes. Sift in the flour, baking powder, and cocoa and whisk in, then whisk in the eggs. Pour the batter into the prepared cake pan.

3 Bake in the preheated oven for 1½ hours, or until risen and firm to the touch. Let cool in the pan for 30 minutes, then turn out and peel off the lining paper. Transfer to a wire rack to cool completely. Decorate with fresh raspberries and chocolate curls and serve.

rich fruit cake

cook: 1 hr 45 mins

prep: 35 mins, plus 1 hr cooling

serves 12

variation

Replace the lemon rind with lime rind and use dried blueberries instead of cranberries, if you prefer.

Serve this moist, fruit-laden cake for a special occasion. It would also make an excellent Christmas or birthday cake.

INGREDIENTS

butter, for greasing

1 cup pitted unsweetened dates

¾ cup no-soak dried prunes

scant 1 cup unsweetened orange juice

2 tbsp molasses

1 tsp finely grated lemon rind

1 tsp finely grated orange rind

1½ cups whole-wheat self-rising flour

1 tsp ground allspice

¾ cup seedless raisins

¾ cup golden raisins

¾ cup currants

¾ cup dried cranberries

3 large eggs, separated

TO DECORATE

1 tbsp apricot jelly, warmed

confectioners' sugar, for dusting

6 oz/175 g sugarpaste

strips of orange rind

strips of lemon rind

cook's tip

For best results, bring the eggs to room temperature before using. If you use very cold eggs, the cake batter may curdle due to the difference in temperature.

1 Grease and line a deep 8 inch/20-cm round cake pan. Chop the dates and prunes and place in a large, heavy-bottom pan. Pour over the orange juice and let simmer for 10 minutes. Remove the pan from the heat and beat the fruit mixture until puréed. Add the molasses and citrus rinds and let cool.

2 Preheat the oven to 325°F/160°C. Sift the flour and spice into a bowl, adding any bran that remains in the strainer. Add the dry fruits. When the date and prune mixture is cool, whisk in the egg yolks. Whisk the egg whites in a clean bowl until stiff. Spoon the fruit mixture into the dry ingredients and mix together.

3 Gently fold in the egg whites. Transfer to the prepared pan and bake in the preheated oven for 1½ hours. Let cool in the pan.

4 Remove the cake from the pan and brush the top with jelly. Dust the counter with confectioners' sugar and roll out the sugarpaste thinly. Lay the sugarpaste over the top of the cake and trim the edges. Decorate with orange and lemon rind.

passion fruit angel cake

serves 8

prep: 20 mins, plus ⏲ **30 mins cooling**

cook: 50–55 mins ♨

This American angel cake is wonderfully light and airy, and its unusual and delicious passion fruit frosting is bound to be a talking point among your guests.

INGREDIENTS

⅔ cup all-purpose flour

scant 1½ cups superfine sugar

8 large egg whites

1 tsp cream of tartar

pinch of salt

1 tsp vanilla extract

2 tbsp warm water

FROSTING

4 passion fruit

2 cups confectioners' sugar

NUTRITIONAL INFORMATION

Calories	288
Protein	. . . . .4g
Carbohydrate	. . . . .72g
Sugars	. . . . .64g
Fat	. . . . .0g
Saturates	. . . . .0g

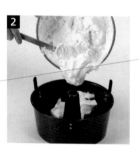

cook's tip

If you do not have an angel cake pan, any other type of cake pan, such as an ungreased tube pan, can be used as a substitute.

1 Preheat the oven to 350°F/180°C. Sift the flour and 2 tablespoons of the sugar onto a sheet of waxed paper. Place the egg whites in a large, spotlessly clean bowl and whisk until frothy, then stir in the cream of tartar and salt. Sprinkle in the vanilla extract and warm water and continue whisking until the egg whites are stiff but not dry. Sift in the remaining sugar, 2 tablespoons at a time, whisking well between each addition, until soft peaks form.

2 Gently fold in the sifted flour and sugar mixture, in several batches. Pour the batter into a nonstick angel cake pan with a funnel. It should be about two-thirds full. Bake in the preheated oven for 50–55 minutes, or until the top is brown and dry to the touch. Turn the pan upside down and let stand until the cake is completely cold. Using a spatula, ease the cake out of the pan and transfer to a serving plate.

3 To make the frosting, cut the passion fruit in half and scoop out the pulp into a strainer set over a bowl. Press the juice from the pulp with a wooden spoon. Stir enough confectioners' sugar into the juice to make a frosting with the consistency of heavy cream. Drizzle the frosting over the cake and let set.

victoria sponge

cook: 25–30 mins　　　**prep: 10 mins, plus 20 mins cooling**　　　serves 8

A Victoria sandwich cake is probably the first cake that most people learn to make and it is usually made by the creaming method, but this is a quicker way, using the all-in-one method.

NUTRITIONAL INFORMATION

Calories 380

Protein 5g

Carbohydrate 48g

Sugars 31g

Fat 20g

Saturates 13g

INGREDIENTS

6 oz/175 g butter, softened,
plus extra for greasing

1¼ cups self-rising flour

1 tsp baking powder

scant 1 cup golden superfine sugar

3 eggs

FILLING

3 tbsp raspberry jelly

2½ cups heavy cream, whipped

16 fresh strawberries, halved

superfine sugar, for dusting

variations

Join the cakes together with lemon curd or another fruit jelly and fresh fruit.

1 Preheat the oven to 350°F/180°C, then grease and line the bottoms of 2 x 8-inch/20-cm sponge cake pans. Sift the flour and baking powder into a bowl and add the butter, sugar, and eggs. Mix together, then beat well until smooth.

2 Divide the batter evenly between the prepared pans and smooth the surfaces. Bake in the preheated oven for 25–30 minutes, or until well risen and golden brown, and the cakes feel springy when lightly pressed.

3 Let cool in the pans for 5 minutes, then turn out and peel off the lining paper. Transfer to wire racks to cool completely. Join the cakes together with the raspberry jelly, whipped heavy cream, and strawberry halves. Sprinkle the superfine sugar on top and serve.

tropical fruit cake

serves 16 **prep: 25 mins, plus** **cook: 2 hrs 30 mins**
9 hrs soaking/cooling

This is the perfect fruit cake to have in the cake pan for any occasion, but it also makes a delicious, slightly lighter alternative to the traditional, rich fruit Christmas cake.

INGREDIENTS

1 lb 7 oz/650 g mixed dry tropical fruit

⅔ cup no-soak dried apricots

⅔ cup golden raisins

⅓ cup rum

7 oz/200 g butter, softened, plus extra for greasing

1 cup golden superfine sugar

3 eggs, beaten

scant 1½ cups all-purpose flour

1 tsp baking powder

1 tsp ground ginger

½ cup dry unsweetened coconut

generous ½ cup coarsely chopped Brazil nuts

generous ½ cup coarsely chopped cashews

1 oz/25 g preserved ginger, finely chopped

NUTRITIONAL INFORMATION

Calories 413

Protein 6g

Carbohydrate 55g

Sugars 43g

Fat 19g

Saturates 9g

variation

Substitute different nuts, such as pecans and walnuts, for the Brazil nuts and cashews, if you prefer.

cook's tip

You may be able to find packages of mixed dry tropical fruit. If not, choose a mixture of fruit such as mango, pineapple, and papaya.

1 Place 14 oz/400 g of the mixed tropical fruit in a food processor with the apricots and process until chopped into small pieces. Transfer to a bowl and add the golden raisins and rum. Cover and let soak for 8 hours, or overnight.

2 Preheat the oven to 300°F/150°C. Grease and line the bottom of a deep 8-inch/20-cm round cake pan. Place the butter and sugar in a bowl and beat together until light and fluffy, then gradually beat in the eggs, adding a little flour toward the end to prevent curdling. Sift in the remaining flour, baking powder, and ground ginger and fold in. Stir in the coconut, two-thirds of the nuts, the preserved ginger, and the soaked fruit. Turn into the prepared pan and smooth the surface.

3 Place the remaining tropical fruit in a food processor and process until coarsely chopped. Scatter over the cake with the remaining nuts. Place the cake in the preheated oven and reduce the temperature to 275°F/140°C. Bake for 2½ hours, or until firm to the touch and a skewer inserted into the center comes out clean. Let cool in the pan for 30 minutes, then turn out and peel off the lining paper. Transfer to a wire rack to cool completely.

carrot & ginger cake

cook: 1 hr 15 mins

prep: 15 mins, plus 1 hr cooling

serves 10

This melt-in-the-mouth version of a favorite cake has a fraction of the fat of the traditional cake.

variations

Replace the raisins with golden raisins or substitute half the raisins with chopped walnuts.

INGREDIENTS

butter, for greasing

1½ cups all-purpose flour

1 tsp baking powder

1 tsp baking soda

2 tsp ground ginger

½ tsp salt

scant ⅞ cup firmly packed brown sugar

8 oz/225 g carrots, grated

2 pieces chopped preserved ginger

1 tbsp grated fresh gingerroot

⅓ cup seedless raisins

2 medium eggs, beaten

3 tbsp corn oil

juice of 1 orange

FROSTING

1 cup lowfat soft cheese

4 tbsp confectioners' sugar

1 tsp vanilla extract

TO DECORATE

grated carrot

finely chopped preserved ginger

ground ginger

cook's tip

When baking cakes it is very important to preheat the oven at least 10 minutes before baking, so the oven reaches the correct temperature before you bake the cake.

1 Preheat the oven to 350°F/180°C. Grease and line an 8-inch/20-cm round cake pan with parchment paper.

2 Sift the flour, baking powder, baking soda, ground ginger, and salt into a large bowl. Stir in the sugar, carrots, preserved ginger, fresh gingerroot, and raisins. Beat the eggs, oil, and orange juice together, then pour into the bowl. Mix the ingredients together well. Spoon the cake batter into the pan and bake in the preheated oven for 1–1¼ hours, or until firm to the touch, or until a skewer inserted into the center of the cake comes out clean. Let the cake cool completely in the pan.

3 To make the frosting, place the soft cheese in a bowl and beat to soften. Sift in the confectioners' sugar and add the vanilla extract. Mix well. Remove the cake from the pan and smooth the frosting over the top. Decorate the cake with a little grated carrot, chopped preserved ginger, and ground ginger and serve.

layer cakes & desserts

Because we no longer eat desserts every day, they have become something of a treat. When you produce a homemade dessert at the end of a meal, it is guaranteed to be met with cries of delight. Your friends and family will really appreciate it when you go to the trouble of making a special dessert.

There are desserts here for every occasion, whether it is a family meal or an elegant dinner party. The recipes in this section range from a stunning Mango & Passion Fruit Pavlova (see page 236) and a rich Manhattan Cheesecake (see page 234) to more homely and comforting puddings, such as Apple & Blackberry Crumble (see page 250) or a magical Lemon Puddle Sponge (see page 247) that makes its own sauce as it cooks.

There are recipes for steamed desserts, but they are not the rib-sticking, stodgy affairs you may remember from school days. Ginger & Lemon Sponges (see page 248) and Sticky Coffee & Walnut Sponges (see page 242) are light and moist. Some old favorites have been given a new twist—upside-down cake has a new look with a tropical fruit topping (see page 243) and bread and butter pudding, made with Italian Panettone, is lifted into a gourmet class (see page 246). Recipes such as Moroccan Orange & Almond Cake (see page 226) or Apple Streusel Cake (see page 230) can be served as cakes as well as desserts. When you produce any of these cakes and desserts, diets are guaranteed to be forgotten.

moroccan orange & almond cake

serves 8

prep: 20 mins, plus ↻
40 mins cooling/standing

cook: 45–50 mins ↻

*This moist almond cake, a rich and unusual treat, is soaked
in a fragrant orange and cardamom syrup.*

INGREDIENTS

4 oz/115 g butter, softened,
plus extra for greasing

1 orange

generous ½ cup golden superfine sugar

2 eggs, beaten

scant 1 cup semolina

generous 1 cup ground almonds

1½ tsp baking powder

confectioners' sugar, for dusting

strained plain yogurt, to serve

SYRUP

1¼ cups orange juice

⅔ cup superfine sugar

8 cardamom pods, crushed

variation

If you like, sprinkle slivered almonds
over the surface of the cake before
dusting it with confectioners' sugar.

cook's tip

Do not be tempted to rush
this cake—make sure that
you give the orange syrup
plenty of time to soak into
the sponge.

1 Preheat the oven to 350°F/180°C. Grease and line the bottom of an 8-inch/20-cm cake pan. Grate the rind from the orange, reserving some for the decoration, and squeeze the juice from one half. Place the butter, orange rind, and superfine sugar in a bowl and beat together until light and fluffy. Gradually beat in the eggs. In a separate bowl, mix the semolina, ground almonds, and baking powder, then fold into the creamed mixture with the orange juice. Spoon the batter into the prepared pan and bake in the preheated oven for 30–40 minutes, or until well risen and a skewer inserted into the center comes out clean. Let cool in the pan for 10 minutes.

2 To make the syrup, place the orange juice, sugar, and cardamom pods in a pan over low heat and stir until the sugar has dissolved. Bring to a boil and simmer for 4 minutes, or until syrupy.

3 Turn the cake out into a deep serving dish. Using a skewer, make holes over the surface of the warm cake. Strain the syrup into a separate bowl and spoon three-quarters of it over the cake, then let stand for 30 minutes. Dust the cake with confectioners' sugar and cut into slices. Serve with the remaining syrup drizzled around, accompanied by strained plain yogurt decorated with the reserved orange rind.

italian bread pudding

serves 4   **prep: 15 mins, plus 30 mins soaking** ⏲   **cook: 25 mins** ⏲

This deliciously rich pudding is cooked with cream and apples and is delicately flavored with orange.

INGREDIENTS

1 tbsp butter, for greasing
2 small dessert apples, peeled, cored and sliced into rings
generous ⅜ cup granulated sugar
2 tbsp white wine
3½ oz/100 g bread, sliced with crusts removed (slightly stale French baguette is ideal)
1¼ cups light cream
2 eggs, beaten
pared rind of 1 orange, cut into short thin sticks

NUTRITIONAL INFORMATION

Calories	.387
Protein	.8g
Carbohydrate	.45g
Sugars	.31g
Fat	.20g
Saturates	.12g

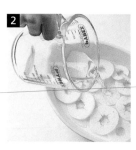

variation

For a change, try adding dry fruit, such as apricots, cherries or dates, to the pudding, if you prefer.

1 Lightly grease a deep 5-cup/1.2-liter ovenproof dish with the butter.

2 Arrange the apple rings in the bottom of the dish. Sprinkle half of the sugar over the apples. Pour the wine over the apples. Add the bread slices, pushing them down with your hands to flatten them slightly.

3 Mix the cream with the eggs, the remaining sugar, and the orange rind together and pour the mixture over the bread. Let soak for 30 minutes.

4 Preheat the oven to 350°F/180°C, then bake the pudding for 25 minutes, or until golden and set.

5 Remove the pudding from the oven, let cool slightly and serve warm.

tuscan puddings

cook: 15 mins   **prep: 20 mins**   **serves 4**

*These baked mini-ricotta puddings are delicious served warm
or chilled and will keep in the refrigerator for 3–4 days.*

NUTRITIONAL INFORMATION	
Calories	.293
Protein	.9g
Carbohydrate	.28g
Sugars	.28g
Fat	.17g
Saturates	.9g

INGREDIENTS

1 tbsp butter, for greasing

½ cup mixed dry fruit

9 oz/250 g ricotta cheese

3 egg yolks

¼ cup superfine sugar

1 tsp cinnamon

finely grated rind of 1 orange, plus

extra to decorate

crème fraîche or sour cream, to serve

cook's tip

Crème fraîche is suitable for cooking, but has the same fat content as heavy cream. It can be made by stirring cultured buttermilk into heavy cream and chilling overnight.

1 Preheat the oven to 350°F/180°C. Lightly grease 4 mini ovenproof bowls or ramekins with the butter. Put the dry fruit in a bowl and cover with warm water. Let soak for 10 minutes.

2 Beat the ricotta cheese with the egg yolks in a bowl. Stir in the superfine sugar, cinnamon, and orange rind and mix to combine. Drain the dry fruit in a strainer set over a bowl. Mix the drained fruit with the ricotta cheese mixture. Spoon the mixture into the bowls or ramekins.

3 Bake the puddings in the preheated oven for 15 minutes. The tops should be firm to the touch but should not have turned brown.

Turn out the puddings and decorate them with grated orange rind. Serve warm or chilled with a spoonful of crème fraîche or sour cream.

apple streusel cake

serves 8 **prep: 20 mins, plus 40 mins cooling** **cook: 1 hr**

This is a cross between a cake and an apple crumble and can be served either as a dessert or as a cake.

INGREDIENTS

4 oz/115 g butter, plus extra for greasing

1 lb/450 g tart cooking apples

1¼ cups self-rising flour

1 tsp ground cinnamon

pinch of salt

generous ½ cup golden superfine sugar

2 eggs

1–2 tbsp milk

confectioners' sugar, for dusting

STREUSEL TOPPING

generous ¾ cup self-rising flour

6 tbsp butter

scant ½ cup golden superfine sugar

NUTRITIONAL INFORMATION

Calories 440

Protein 5g

Carbohydrate 58g

Sugars 31g

Fat 23g

Saturates 14g

variation

As an alternative to apples, you can substitute fresh rhubarb, gooseberries, or pears, if you prefer.

cook's tip

Try to work quickly when you make the cake batter in Step 2, so the sliced apples do not have time to turn brown when exposed to the air.

1 Preheat the oven to 350°F/180°C, then grease a 9-inch/23-cm springform cake pan. To make the streusel topping, sift the flour into a bowl and rub in the butter until the mixture resembles coarse crumbs. Stir in the sugar and set aside.

2 Peel, core, and thinly slice the apples. To make the cake, sift the flour into a bowl with the cinnamon and salt. Place the butter and sugar in a separate bowl and beat together until light and fluffy. Gradually beat in the eggs, adding a little of the flour mixture with the last addition of egg. Gently fold in half the remaining flour mixture, then fold in the rest with the milk.

3 Spoon the batter into the prepared pan and smooth the top. Cover with the sliced apples and sprinkle the streusel topping evenly over the top. Bake in the preheated oven for 1 hour, or until browned and firm to the touch. Let cool in the pan before opening the sides. Dust the cake with confectioners' sugar before serving.

eve's pudding

serves 6   **prep: 15 mins**   **cook: 45 mins**

This is a popular family favorite pudding with soft apples on the bottom and a light buttery sponge on top.

INGREDIENTS

6 tbsp butter, plus extra for greasing

1 lb/450 g tart cooking apples, peeled, cored, and sliced

generous ⅜ cup granulated sugar

1 tbsp lemon juice

scant ⅓ cup golden raisins

generous ⅜ cup superfine sugar

1 egg, beaten

1 cup self-rising flour

3 tbsp milk

2 tbsp slivered almonds

custard or heavy cream, to serve

NUTRITIONAL INFORMATION

Calories	365
Protein	5g
Carbohydrate	58g
Sugars	40g
Fat	14g
Saturates	7g

cook's tip

To increase the almond flavour of this pudding, add a generous ¼ cup ground almonds with the flour in Step 2.

1 Preheat the oven to 350°F/180°C. Grease a 3½-cup/850-ml ovenproof dish with butter. Mix the apples with the sugar, lemon juice, and golden raisins. Spoon the mixture into the greased dish.

2 Beat the butter and superfine sugar together in a bowl until pale. Add the egg, a little at a time.

Carefully fold in the flour and stir in the milk to give a soft, dropping consistency.

3 Spread the mixture over the apples and sprinkle with the slivered almonds.

4 Bake the pudding in the preheated oven for 40–45 minutes, or until the sponge is golden brown.

Serve piping hot, accompanied by homemade custard or heavy cream.

queen of puddings

cook: 50 mins

prep: 15 mins, plus 15 mins standing

serves 8

A slightly different version of this favorite is made with the addition of orange rind and marmalade to give a delicious citrus flavor.

NUTRITIONAL INFORMATION

Calories 289

Protein 6g

Carbohydrate 50g

Sugars 46g

Fat 8g

Saturates 4g

INGREDIENTS

2 tbsp butter, plus extra for greasing

2½ cups milk

generous 1 cup superfine sugar

finely grated rind of 1 orange

4 eggs, separated

1⅜ cups fresh bread crumbs

salt

6 tbsp orange marmalade

cook's tip

Try to choose a strongly flavored marmalade so that its richness is not totally overpowered by the flavors of all the spices.

1 Grease a 6-cup/1.5-liter ovenproof dish with butter.

2 To make the custard, heat the milk in a pan with the butter, ¼ cup of the superfine sugar, and the grated orange rind until just warm.

3 Whisk the egg yolks in a bowl. Gradually pour the warm milk over the eggs, whisking constantly. Stir the bread crumbs into the bowl, then transfer the mixture to the dish and let stand for 15 minutes.

4 Preheat the oven to 350°F/180°C, then bake the pudding for

20–25 minutes, until the custard has just set. Remove the custard from the oven, but do not turn the oven off.

5 To make the meringue, whisk the egg whites with a pinch of salt in a spotlessly clean, greasefree bowl until soft peaks form. Whisk in the remaining sugar, a little at a time. Spread the

orange marmalade over the cooked custard. Top with the meringue, spreading it right to the edges of the dish. Return the pudding to the oven and bake for an additional 20 minutes, or until the meringue is crisp and golden.

manhattan cheesecake

serves 8–10

prep: 20 mins, plus ⏲
10 hrs cooling/chilling

cook: 35 mins ⏲

*This is a classic American baked cheesecake, given a splash of
color with a traditional fruity blueberry topping.*

INGREDIENTS

sunflower or corn oil, for brushing

6 tbsp butter

7 oz/200 g graham crackers, crushed

1¾ cups cream cheese

2 large eggs

scant ¾ cup superfine sugar

1½ tsp vanilla extract

scant 2 cups sour cream

BLUEBERRY TOPPING

¼ cup superfine sugar

4 tbsp water

9 oz/250 g fresh blueberries

1 tsp arrowroot

NUTRITIONAL INFORMATION

Calories 658

Protein 7g

Carbohydrate 48g

Sugars 33g

Fat 50g

Saturates 30g

variation

As an alternative to blueberries,
try raspberries, black currants, or
cranberries for the topping.

cook's tip

If possible, it is best to let
the cheesecake chill in the
refrigerator overnight at
the end of Step 2.

1 Preheat the oven to
375°F/190°C. Brush an
8-inch/20-cm springform pan
with oil. Melt the butter in a
pan over low heat. Stir in the
crackers, then spread in the
pan. Place the cream cheese,
eggs, ½ cup of the sugar, and
½ teaspoon of the vanilla
extract in a food processor.
Process until smooth. Pour
over the cracker layer and

smooth the top. Place on a
baking sheet and bake for
20 minutes, or until set.
Remove from the oven and let
stand for 20 minutes. Leave
the oven switched on.

2 Mix the cream with
the remaining sugar
and vanilla extract in a bowl.
Spoon over the cheesecake.
Return it to the oven for

10 minutes, let cool, then chill
in the refrigerator for 8 hours,
or overnight.

3 To make the topping,
place the sugar in a pan
with half of the water over low
heat and stir until the sugar
has dissolved. Increase the
heat, add the blueberries,
cover, and cook for a few
minutes, or until they start

to soften. Remove from the
heat. Mix the arrowroot and
remaining water in a bowl,
add to the fruit, and stir until
smooth. Return to low heat.
Cook until the juice thickens
and turns translucent. Let cool.
Remove the cheesecake from
the pan 1 hour before serving.
Spoon the fruit on top and chill
until ready to serve.

mango & passion fruit pavlova

serves 8

prep: 30 mins, plus 1 hour cooling

cook: 1 hr 15 mins– 1 hr 30 mins

The pavlova is sometimes described as Australia's national dish. It is claimed to have been invented in 1935 by an Australian chef who named it after the Russian ballerina, Anna Pavlova.

INGREDIENTS

3 egg whites

scant 1 cup superfine sugar

1 tsp cornstarch, sifted

1 tsp white wine vinegar

½ tsp vanilla extract

FILLING

1¼ cups heavy cream

2 mangoes

4 passion fruit

NUTRITIONAL INFORMATION	
Calories	.285
Protein	.2g
Carbohydrate	.30g
Sugars	.30g
Fat	.18g
Saturates	.11g

variation

Vary the fruit used in the topping according to what is available. In the summer, raspberries, strawberries, and red currants make a stunning topping.

1 Preheat the oven to 250°F/120°C. Line a cookie sheet with nonstick parchment paper and draw a 9-inch/23-cm circle on the paper. Turn the paper over. Place the egg whites in a spotlessly clean bowl and whisk until stiff. Whisk in the sugar, one-third at a time, whisking well between each addition until stiff and glossy.

Fold in the cornstarch, vinegar, and vanilla extract.

2 Pile the meringue onto the marked circle and make a hollow in the center. Bake in the preheated oven for 1¼–1½ hours, or until lightly colored and dry, but a little soft in the center. Turn off the oven and let the meringue stand in the oven until cold. Peel off the parchment paper. Do not worry if the meringue crumbles slightly at this stage.

3 To make the filling, place the cream in a bowl and whip until thick, then spoon on top of the pavlova. Cut the mangoes in half and slice the flesh into cubes. Pile the cubes on top of the cream. Cut the passion fruit in half and scoop out the flesh on top of the mango. Serve the pavlova immediately.

strawberry & almond roulade

cook: 15 mins

prep: 20 mins, plus 30 mins cooling

serves 8

A light, flourless almond sponge is wrapped round a filling of strawberries and mascarpone cheese in this variation on a classic, popular dessert.

NUTRITIONAL INFORMATION	
Calories	.460
Protein	.11g
Carbohydrate	.33g
Sugars	.32g
Fat	.33g
Saturates	.13g

INGREDIENTS

butter, for greasing

6 eggs

1 cup golden superfine sugar

2 tsp baking powder

2 cups ground almonds

confectioners' sugar, for dusting

FILLING

⅔ cup mascarpone cheese

⅔ cup heavy cream

3 cups fresh strawberries

variation

Raspberries will also complement the flavor of almonds, and make a good alternative to strawberries.

1 Preheat the oven to 350°F/180°C. Grease and line the bottom and sides of a 15 x 10-inch/38 x 25-cm jelly roll pan. Separate the eggs, placing the whites in a large bowl and the yolks in a separate bowl. Add the sugar to the yolks and whisk together until pale and thick. Place the baking powder and ground almonds in a bowl and mix together. Stir gently into the yolk mixture, taking care not to overmix. Whisk the egg whites until they form soft peaks and then carefully fold in the egg whites.

2 Spread in the pan and bake in the preheated oven for 15 minutes, or until firm. Cover with a clean dish towel and let cool in the pan.

3 Place a sheet of waxed paper on the counter and dust thickly with confectioners' sugar. Turn the roulade out on to the paper and peel off the lining paper. Spread the cream over the roulade and scatter the chopped strawberries over. Roll up and serve, cut into slices, within 1–2 hours of assembling.

To make the filling, place the mascarpone cheese and cream in a bowl and stir together to give a spreading consistency. Place half the strawberries in a separate bowl and mash. Coarsely chop the remainder and set aside. Stir the mashed strawberries into the cream.

bread & butter pudding

cook: 1 hr

prep: 35 mins, plus 20–30 mins standing

serves 6

Everyone has their own favorite recipe for this dish. This one has added marmalade and grated apples for a rich taste.

INGREDIENTS

5 tbsp butter, softened

4–5 slices of white or brown bread

4 tbsp chunky orange marmalade

grated rind of 1 lemon

½–¾ cup raisins

¼ cup chopped candied peel

1 tsp ground cinnamon

1 tart cooking apple, peeled, cored, and coarsely grated

generous ⅜ cup brown sugar

3 eggs

scant 2½ cups milk

2 tbsp raw brown sugar

variations

Substitute the raisins with the same amount of golden raisins and use allspice instead of ground cinnamon.

cook's tip

Cut the crusts off the slices of bread before fitting them into the dish, if you prefer. If the top is starting to brown too quickly, then cover with a piece of foil.

1 Use the butter to grease an ovenproof dish and to spread on the slices of bread, then spread the bread with the marmalade.

2 Place a layer of bread in the bottom of the dish and sprinkle with the lemon rind, half the raisins, half the candied peel, half the cinnamon, all of the apple, and half the brown sugar. Add another layer of bread, cutting the slices so that they fit the dish.

3 Sprinkle over most of the remaining raisins and the remaining candied peel, cinnamon, and brown sugar, sprinkling it evenly over the bread. Top with a final layer of bread, again cutting to fit the dish. Lightly beat the eggs and milk together, then carefully strain the mixture over the bread in the dish. If time allows, let stand for 20–30 minutes.

4 Preheat the oven to 400°F/200°C. Sprinkle the top of the pudding with the raw brown sugar and scatter over the remaining raisins and cook in the preheated oven for 50–60 minutes, or until risen and golden brown. Serve immediately if serving hot or let cool completely and serve cold.

peach melba meringue roulade

serves 8 **prep: 25 mins, plus 15 mins cooling** **cook: 45–50 mins**

This cloud of meringue is a dessert to die for—crunchy on the outside and gooey within. The meringue can be made up to 8 hours before being filled, and once assembled, the roulade will keep for up to 2 days in the refrigerator.

NUTRITIONAL INFORMATION

Calories 428

Protein 4g

Carbohydrate 63g

Sugars 62g

Fat 19g

Saturates 12g

INGREDIENTS

sunflower or corn oil, for brushing

COULIS

12 oz/350 g fresh raspberries

generous 1 cup confectioners' sugar

MERINGUE

2 tsp cornstarch

1½ cups superfine sugar

5 large egg whites

1 tsp cider vinegar

FILLING

3 peaches, peeled, pitted, and chopped (see Cook's Tip)

9 oz/250 g fresh raspberries

generous ¾ cup sour cream

⅔ cup heavy cream

variation

When fresh peaches are out of season, canned peaches may be used instead. Thawed frozen raspberries may be used instead of fresh.

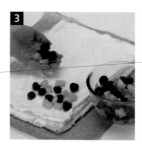

cook's tip

To peel and pit the peaches, place them in a bowl, cover with boiling water, and let stand for 30 seconds. Drain and plunge into a bowl of cold water. Peel off the skins, cut in half, and remove the pits.

1 Preheat the oven to 300°F/150°C. Oil a 14 x 10-inch/35 x 25-cm jelly roll pan and line with nonstick parchment paper. To make the coulis, process the raspberries and confectioners' sugar to a purée. Press through a strainer into a bowl and set aside. To make the meringue, sift the cornstarch into a bowl and stir in the sugar. In a separate, spotlessly clean bowl, whisk the egg whites into stiff peaks, then whisk in the vinegar. Gradually whisk in the cornstarch and sugar mixture until stiff and glossy.

2 Spread the mixture evenly in the lined pan, leaving a ½-inch/1-cm border. Bake in the center of the oven for 20 minutes, then reduce the heat to 225°F/110°C and cook for an additional 25–30 minutes, or until puffed up. Remove from the oven. Let cool for 15 minutes. Turn out onto parchment paper.

3 To make the filling, place the peaches in a bowl with the raspberries. Add 2 tablespoons of the coulis and mix. In a separate bowl, whisk the sour cream and heavy cream together until thick. Spread over the meringue. Scatter the fruit over the cream, leaving a 1¼-inch/3-cm border at one short edge. Using the parchment paper, lift and roll the meringue, starting at the short edge without the border, ending up seam-side down. Lift onto a plate and serve with the coulis.

sticky coffee & walnut sponges

serves 6   **prep: 20 mins** ⏱   **cook: 30–40 mins** ⏱

These delightful little coffee sponges with a butterscotch sauce are guaranteed to delight your guests.

INGREDIENTS

2 oz/55 g butter, softened,

plus extra for greasing

1 tbsp instant coffee powder

generous 1 cup self-rising flour

1 tsp ground cinnamon

¼ cup brown sugar, sifted

2 large eggs, beaten

⅓ cup finely chopped walnuts

BUTTERSCOTCH SAUCE

scant ¼ cup coarsely chopped walnuts

2 oz/55 g butter

¼ cup brown sugar

⅔ cup heavy cream

NUTRITIONAL INFORMATION

Calories	.520
Protein	.7g
Carbohydrate	.39g
Sugars	.21g
Fat	.38g
Saturates	.19g

cook's tip

This could be cooked as one large sponge, in which case the batter should be put into a heatproof bowl, covered, and steamed for 1½ hours.

1 Preheat the oven to 375°F/190°C, then grease 6 individual metal dessert cups. Dissolve the coffee powder in 2 tablespoons of boiling water and set aside. Sift the flour and cinnamon into a bowl. Place the butter and sugar in a separate bowl and beat together until light and fluffy. Gradually beat in the eggs. Add a little flour if the mixture shows signs of curdling. Fold in half the flour and cinnamon mixture, then fold in the remaining flour and cinnamon, alternately with the coffee. Stir in the walnuts.

2 Divide the batter between the metal cups. Place a piece of buttered aluminum foil over each cup and secure with an elastic band. Stand the cups in a roasting pan and pour in enough boiling water to reach halfway up the sides of the cups. Cover the roasting pan with a tent of foil, folding it under the rim.

3 Bake the sponges in the preheated oven for 30–40 minutes, or until well risen and firm to the touch.

4 Meanwhile, make the sauce. Place all of the ingredients in a pan over low heat and stir until melted and blended. Bring to a simmer, then remove from the heat. Turn the sponges out onto a serving plate, spoon over the hot sauce, and serve.

upside-down tropical fruit cake

🕒 cook: 50–60 mins   ⏲ prep: 25 mins, plus 10 mins standing   serves 8

This sticky, fruity cake is delicious served hot with ice cream, or it can be left to cool and served cold.

NUTRITIONAL INFORMATION

Calories 472

Protein 5g

Carbohydrate 58g

Sugars 41g

Fat 26g

Saturates 16g

INGREDIENTS

6 oz/175 g butter, softened, plus extra for greasing

scant 1 cup brown sugar

3 eggs

1¼ cups self-rising flour

1 tsp ground allspice

TOPPING

2 oz/55 g butter, softened

¼ cup brown sugar

2 bananas

1 small pineapple

1 mango

cook's tip

If time is limited and you want to speed up the preparation time for this recipe, the cake batter can be mixed in a food processor.

1 Preheat the oven to 350°F/180°C. Grease a deep 8-inch/20-cm round cake pan.

2 To make the topping, spread the butter evenly over the bottom of the pan and sprinkle the sugar on top. Peel the bananas and slice thickly, then peel the pineapple and mango and cut into chunks. Mix the fruit together and pile evenly over the bottom of the pan.

3 To make the cake, place the butter, sugar, and eggs in a bowl and sift in the flour and allspice. Beat together until light and fluffy, then spread the batter over the fruit. Bake in the preheated oven for 50 minutes–1 hour, or until well risen and firm to the touch. Let stand in the pan for 10 minutes, then loosen the edges with a spatula and turn out onto a serving plate.

german noodle pudding

cook: 50 mins **prep: 10 mins** **serves 4**

NUTRITIONAL INFORMATION

Calories 719

Protein 20g

Carbohydrate 62g

Sugars 28g

Fat 45g

Saturates 25g

This rich and satisfying pudding is a traditional Jewish recipe that will quickly become popular with all the family.

INGREDIENTS

4 tbsp butter, plus extra for greasing	1 tsp vanilla extract
6 oz/175 g ribbon egg noodles	pinch of ground cinnamon
½ cup cream cheese	1 tsp grated lemon rind
1 cup cottage cheese	¼ cup slivered almonds
generous ⅜ cup superfine sugar	¼ cup dry white bread crumbs
2 eggs, lightly beaten	confectioners' sugar, for dusting
½ cup sour cream	

variation

Although not authentic, you could add 3 tablespoons of raisins with the lemon rind in Step 2, if you like.

cook's tip

When cooking the almonds, keep stirring and watching them because they may burn easily. Remove the skillet from the heat as soon as the almonds turn pale golden.

1 Preheat the oven to 350°F/180°C. Grease an ovenproof dish with a little butter. Bring a pan of water to a boil. Add the noodles, return to a boil, and cook until almost tender. Drain and set aside.

2 Beat the cream cheese, cottage cheese, and superfine sugar together in a large bowl until the mixture is smooth. Beat in the eggs, a little at a time. Stir in the sour cream, vanilla extract, cinnamon, and lemon rind and fold in the noodles. Transfer the mixture to the prepared dish and smooth the surface.

3 Melt the butter in a small skillet over low heat. Add the almonds and cook, stirring constantly, for 1–1½ minutes, or until they are lightly colored. Remove the skillet from the heat and stir the bread crumbs into the almonds.

4 Sprinkle the almond and bread crumb mixture evenly over the pudding and bake in the preheated oven for 35–40 minutes, or until just set. Dust the top with a little sifted confectioners' sugar and serve.

panettone dessert

serves 6   **prep: 15 mins, plus 1 hr standing**   **cook: 40 mins**

This is a variation of bread and butter pudding, made with panettone, an Italian cross between bread and cake.

INGREDIENTS

3 tbsp butter, softened,
plus extra for greasing

9 oz/250 g panettone, cut into slices

scant 1 cup milk

scant 1 cup heavy cream

1 vanilla bean, split

3 eggs

generous ½ cup golden superfine sugar

2 tbsp apricot jelly, warmed
and strained

NUTRITIONAL INFORMATION

Calories	.496
Protein	.9g
Carbohydrate	.49g
Sugars	.34g
Fat	.31g
Saturates	.17g

cook's tip

The vanilla bean used in this recipe may be rinsed clean and patted dry with paper towels and used again in another recipe.

1 Grease a 3½-cup shallow ovenproof dish. Butter the slices of panettone and arrange in the dish. Place the milk, cream, and vanilla bean in a pan over low heat until the mixture reaches boiling point. Place the eggs and sugar in a bowl and beat together, then pour in the milk mixture and beat together.

2 Pour the custard through a strainer over the buttered panettone. Let stand for 1 hour so that the panettone soaks up the custard. Preheat the oven to 325°F/160°C.

3 Bake the dessert in the preheated oven for 40 minutes, then drizzle the apricot jelly over the top. If the top crusts of the dessert are not crisp and golden, heat under a preheated hot broiler for 1 minute before serving.

lemon puddle sponge

🕐 **cook: 50 mins–1 hr**   🕐 **prep: 15 mins**   **serves 6**

This is a delicious hot sponge, complete with its own sauce, which forms underneath the sponge while baking.

NUTRITIONAL INFORMATION

Calories 360

Protein 8g

Carbohydrate 39g

Sugars 34g

Fat 20g

Saturates 12g

INGREDIENTS

3½ oz/100 g butter, softened,
plus extra for greasing

scant 1 cup golden superfine sugar

grated rind and juice of 2 lemons

4 eggs

⅓ cup all-purpose flour

1¾ cups milk

confectioners' sugar, for dusting

cook's tip

Lemons vary in the amount of juice they produce, so if you think your lemons are not very juicy, use 3 in this recipe. When using the rind in a recipe, try to find unwaxed lemons.

1 Preheat the oven to 350°F/180°C. Grease a 4-cup ovenproof dish. Place the butter, sugar, and lemon rind in a bowl and beat together until light and fluffy. Separate the eggs, placing the whites in a spotlessly clean bowl, and beat the yolks into the creamed butter and sugar with the flour and lemon juice.

2 Gradually stir the milk into the lemon batter. Whisk the egg whites until stiff peaks form, then gently fold into the batter. Pour into the prepared dish. The batter should come halfway up the sides.

3 Stand the dish in a roasting pan and pour in enough hot water to reach a depth of 1 inch/2.5 cm. Bake in the preheated oven for 50 minutes–1 hour, or until well risen and golden. Let cool for 5 minutes, then dust with sifted confectioners' sugar and serve.

ginger & lemon sponges

serves 8   **prep: 20 mins**   **cook: 30–40 mins**

These little puddings are very light and will not fill you up too much if you serve them at the end of a heavy meal.

INGREDIENTS

4 oz/115 g butter, softened, plus extra for greasing

2 lemons

3 oz/85 g drained preserved ginger, chopped, plus 1 tbsp ginger syrup from the jar

2 tbsp corn syrup

1¼ cups self-rising flour

2 tsp ground ginger

generous ½ cup golden superfine sugar

2 eggs, beaten

3–4 tbsp milk

vanilla custard, to serve

variation

If you prefer, you can serve the sponges with vanilla ice cream rather than custard.

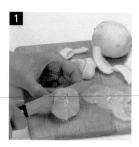

cook's tip

When grating the rind from the lemons, be careful not to grate any of the white pith underneath it, otherwise the finished dish will taste bitter.

1 Preheat the oven to 325°F/160°C. Grease 8 individual metal dessert cups. Grate the rind from the lemons and reserve in a bowl. Remove all the pith from one of the lemons and slice the flesh into 8 thin circles. Squeeze the juice from half of the second lemon and reserve. Place the ginger, syrup, corn syrup, and 1 teaspoon of the lemon juice in a bowl and mix together.

2 Divide the mixture between the prepared dessert cups. Place a slice of lemon in the bottom of each cup. Sift the flour and ground ginger into a bowl. Place the butter and sugar in a separate bowl and beat together until light and fluffy. Gradually beat in the eggs, then fold in the flour mixture and add enough milk to give a soft dropping consistency. Stir in the reserved grated lemon rind and the preserved ginger.

3 Divide the batter between the prepared cups. Place a piece of buttered foil over each cup and secure with an elastic band. Stand the cups in a roasting pan and pour in enough boiling water to reach halfway up the sides of the cups. Cover the roasting pan with a tent of foil, folding it under the rim. Bake in the oven for 30–40 minutes, or until well risen and firm to the touch. Turn the sponges out onto a serving dish and serve with vanilla custard.

apple & blackberry crumble

serves 4   **prep: 15 mins** ⏲   **cook: 40–45 mins** ♨

*A crumble is one of the easiest desserts to make
and it is always a popular end to any family meal.*

INGREDIENTS

2 lb/900 g tart cooking apples,
peeled and sliced

10½ oz/300 g blackberries, fresh or frozen

¼ cup brown sugar

1 tsp ground cinnamon

custard or pouring cream, to serve

CRUMBLE

⅔ cup self-rising flour

⅔ cup whole-wheat all-purpose flour

4 oz/115 g butter

¼ cup raw brown sugar

NUTRITIONAL INFORMATION

Calories 530

Protein 6g

Carbohydrate 76g

Sugars 47g

Fat 25g

Saturates 16g

---

variation

Sprinkle a handful of chopped or
slivered almonds over the crumble
before baking, if you like.

---

cook's tip

When making a crumble, keep
rubbing in the butter until the
crumbs are quite coarse. This
ensures that the crumble will
be crunchy.

1 Preheat the oven to 400°F/200°C. Peel and core the apples and cut into chunks. Place in a bowl with the blackberries, sugar, and cinnamon and mix together, then transfer to an ovenproof baking dish.

2 To make the crumble, sift the self-rising flour into a bowl and stir in the whole-wheat flour. Add the butter and rub it in with your fingers until the mixture resembles coarse bread crumbs. Stir in the sugar.

3 Spread the crumble over the apples and bake in the preheated oven for 40–45 minutes, or until the apples are soft and the crumble is golden brown and crisp. Serve with custard or pouring cream.

blackberry pudding

serves 4 **prep: 15 mins** ⏱ **cook: 30 mins** ⏱

A delicious dessert to make when blackberries are in abundance. If blackberries are unavailable, try using currants or gooseberries.

INGREDIENTS

6 tbsp butter, melted, plus extra
for greasing
1 lb/450 g blackberries
generous ⅜ cup superfine sugar
1 egg
generous ⅜ cup brown sugar
8 tbsp milk
generous ⅝ cup self-rising flour
sugar, for sprinkling

NUTRITIONAL INFORMATION

Calories 455

Protein 7g

Carbohydrate 70g

Sugars 47g

Fat 18g

Saturates 11g

variation

You can add 2 tablespoons of unsweetened cocoa to the batter in Step 3, if you prefer a chocolate flavor.

1 Preheat the oven to 350°F/180°C. Lightly grease a large 3½-cup/900-ml ovenproof dish with butter.

2 Gently mix the blackberries and superfine sugar together in a large bowl, until combined. Transfer the blackberry and sugar mixture to the dish.

3 Beat the egg and brown sugar in a separate mixing bowl. Stir in the melted butter and milk, then sift in the flour and fold together lightly with a figure-of-eight movement to form a smooth batter.

4 Carefully spread the batter over the blackberry and sugar mixture in the ovenproof dish. Bake the pudding in the preheated oven for 25–30 minutes, or until the topping is firm and golden. Sprinkle the pudding with sugar and serve hot.

raspberry shortcake

cook: 15 mins

prep: 15 mins, plus 30 mins cooling

serves 8

For this lovely summery dessert, two crisp circles of shortbread are sandwiched together with fresh raspberries and whipped cream.

NUTRITIONAL INFORMATION

Calories	.496
Protein	.4g
Carbohydrate	.30g
Sugars	.14g
Fat	.41g
Saturates	.26g

INGREDIENTS

3½ oz/100 g butter, cut into cubes, plus extra for greasing

scant 1 cup self-rising flour

generous ⅜ cup superfine sugar

1 egg yolk

1 tbsp rose water

all-purpose flour, for dusting

2½ cups whipping cream, lightly whipped

1 cup raspberries, plus a few extra to decorate

TO DECORATE

confectioners' sugar

cook's tip

If you like, the shortcake can be made a few days in advance and stored in an airtight container until required.

1 Preheat the oven to 375°F/190°C. Lightly grease 2 cookie sheets with the butter.

2 To make the shortcake, sift the flour into a large bowl. Add the butter and rub it into the flour with your fingertips until the mixture resembles bread crumbs. Stir the sugar, egg yolk, and rose water into the mixture and mix together with your fingers to form a soft dough. Divide the dough in half.

3 Roll each piece of dough to an 8-inch/20-cm circle on a floured counter. Carefully lift each one with the rolling pin onto a prepared cookie sheet. Crimp the edges of the dough.

4 Bake in the preheated oven for 15 minutes, or until lightly golden. Transfer the shortcakes to a wire rack and let cool completely.

5 Mix the whipped cream with the raspberries and spoon the mixture on top of one of the shortcakes, spreading it out evenly. Top with the other shortcake round, dust with a little confectioners' sugar and decorate with the extra raspberries.

index